NETWORK LIKE YOU MEAN IT

NETWORK LIKE YOU MEAN IT

The Definitive Handbook for Business and Personal Networking

Andrea R. Nierenberg

Vice President, Publisher: Tim Moore
Associate Publisher and Director of Marketing: Amy Neidlinger
Development Editor: Russ Hall
Operations Specialist: Jodi Kemper
Cover Designer: Chuti Prasertsith
Managing Editor: Kristy Hart
Project Editor: Katie Matejka
Copy Editor: Krista Hansing
Proofreader: Chuck Hutchinson
Indexer: Lisa Stumpf
Compositor: Nonie Ratcliff
Manufacturing Buyer: Dan Uhrig

Pearson offers excellent discounts on this book when ordered in quantity for bulk purchases or special sales. For more information, please contact U.S. Corporate and Government Sales, 1-800-382-3419, corpsales@pearsontechgroup.com. For sales outside the U.S., please contact International Sales at international@pearsoned.com.

Printed in the United States of America

First Printing December 2013

ISBN-10: 0-13-374290-3
ISBN-13: 978-0-13-374290-9

Pearson Education LTD.
Pearson Education Australia PTY, Limited.
Pearson Education Singapore, Pte. Ltd.
Pearson Education Asia, Ltd.
Pearson Education Canada, Ltd.
Pearson Educación de Mexico, S.A. de C.V.
Pearson Education—Japan
Pearson Education Malaysia, Pte. Ltd.

Library of Congress Control Number: 2013949116

To my wonderful parents, Molly and Paul,
who always taught me life's greatest lessons.

And to all of those who have made networking
a tool for their success in life.

Contents

Part 2   Grow (Building on Your Strengths) 93

Acknowledgments

Thank you to Tim Moore, Publisher of Pearson Education, for his hands-on ability to make things happen and for his superior skills that have made many books like this very successful.

A huge thank you to all of the terrific people at Pearson who contributed their amazing skills in pulling this book together.

Thank you to Russ Hall for his gift in writing and extraordinary editorial talents.

Thank you to Sean Stowers of Pearson Learning Solutions who thinks out of the box and was the one who "networked" me into the organization and opened the door.

Thank you to Linda Schuler for her excellent administrative and savvy skills.

And a warm and sincere thank you to all the wonderful people in my life who shared their stories and experiences that I incorporated into this book. The list goes on and on—and I thank every single one of you from the bottom of my heart.

Thanks so much to all of you.

About the Author

Andrea R. Nierenberg, author, speaker, networking strategist, and business coach and consultant is the force behind The Nierenberg Consulting Group. Called a "networking success story" by the *Wall Street Journal,* Andrea founded The Nierenberg Consulting Group in 1993.

Her firm provides training in networking, sales, customer service, and presentation skills—all skills that impact the bottom line.

With a stellar 30 years as a leader in sales and marketing, Andrea is an in-demand business expert both at home and abroad. Her firm partners with an array of the world's leading financial and media industry businesses.

Introduction

May I have your card?" I asked Melinda, a woman I met at an event. She had told me she was in real estate, a business, like most, in which everyone is constantly "networking" for new clients. I offered to send her a copy of my first book on networking.

She didn't have her card with her, yet she did tell me her name and where she worked. At the end of the evening, we said goodbye, and I'm sure she thought I'd forget to send the book (follow-up sometimes falls through the cracks). I wrote down her name and company info on my electronic notepad (an important networking tool). The next morning, I called her company, found out she worked in the main office (the company has 10 branch offices), and sent her a copy.

A week later, she emailed me and wrote, "Thank you. I'm pleasantly surprised for three reasons." What were they?

1. I'd remembered her name and her company (I'd immediately recorded it on my phone.)

2. I'd found her company address and her specific location. (I was resourceful, and technology makes it so easy.)

3. I'd sent her the book (I'd followed through).

She was so impressed that she told me she'd give the book to Bill, the vice president of sales, with the hope that he might invite me to speak with the other agents in her firm. A week later, Bill left me a voicemail and invited me to meet with him to discuss the possibility of speaking about networking to 200 agents. Before my next step, I sent an email to

Melinda (her preferred method of communication) to thank her, as my original contact.

I then looked up Bill on both LinkedIn and the firm website, to do my homework before we connected. I learned about his background, and I prepared some conversation starters for our meeting.

Fast-forward to the day of the workshop. My meeting with Bill had gone well. I looked around the large room and saw three people I recognized. One was a neighbor of mine, Diane. We had always smiled and said hello, but we'd never formally met. Now Diane and I are both friends and working colleagues, and since I'm a referral broker, I always send connections her way to anyone looking for a real estate agent. I recognized another woman from my yoga class. Now when we see each other in class, we always greet each other warmly. The third person was someone I'd previously seen in a store speaking rudely to a salesperson. Needless to say, I'd be hesitant to refer her to any of my clients. We all have bad days, yet in the world of business networking and in life, the golden rule always applies.

So because of that chance meeting at the industry event, and because I had taken the opportunity to follow up, was resourceful, and had thanked my networking contacts in the firm, I landed the opportunity and ended up working with several of its branches.

It all began when I went to the event prepared with these tools:

- Networking toolkits
- Primed "networking awareness"
- A system for follow-up and follow-through

I've also continued to thank Melinda and Bill every time I'm referred to another office. Why? Because they were the first to recommend my service, and it keeps me on their radar. (By the way, in case you're wondering, I immediately went back and thanked my friend, Bruce, who had invited me to the event, and have kept him posted about my success with the firm.)

In fact, I make it a practice before any engagement to say "thank you" to *all* the people who've referred me, which is part of my "thank you chain" (more about that later). And I always thank them by their preferred method—email, voicemail, text, or social media.

I've seen over and over how personal contacts can turn into professional ones. In fact, the art of effective networking is absolutely vital to building solid business relationships; finding, growing, and keeping your business; and enhancing your life.

To make sure this book covers everything people need to know about networking, I asked people in my network to share their questions about networking. Here's what they asked and what you will learn in this book:

- How do I start a conversation with someone I find intimidating?
- How do I ask tough questions tactfully?
- How do I start and exit a conversation at internal and external business events?
- How do I "network" with someone I might not like but who is key in the department or industry?
- What are some topics to avoid?
- What are examples of great opening lines, icebreakers, and small talk when I'm networking?
- How do I follow up?
- How do I establish and create advocates and referral opportunities?
- How do I know when I'm networking?
- Where can I find a systematic approach to networking?
- How can I keep all my contacts organized and easy to reach?
- How can I continue to find, keep, and grow my business all the time?
- How do I develop my own "self-brand"?

These kinds of questions always come up, along with remarks about how networking can be scary or cringe-worthy. That might be the reason you shy away from the very skills that can help you both personally and professionally.

Before you go further, take a minute to answer these questions yourself:

- How did you find out about your current (or any previous) job?
- How did you meet your spouse?
- How did you choose your neighborhood?
- How do you decide on a vacation spot and accommodations?
- How did you get your last promotion?
- How do you find clients for your business?
- How did you find your doctor, dentist, accountant, day care provider, health club, or favorite restaurant?

When you sought advice from people you knew, when someone introduced you to a person who could help you, or when someone championed your cause, you were networking. Have you done the same for others? If so, you were networking. You might not have realized it, but that is the essence of networking.

What you might lack is a systematic approach to networking, a way of life that can help you draw upon the vast number of people with whom you come in contact, by choice or by chance.

If you are already a seasoned professional and consider yourself a good networker, some of what you'll find in this book will be a refresher course, a checklist for following up, and a guide to new techniques for building your network and keeping it growing. If you're new to the strategies of reaching out to your personal and professional contacts and making them part of your business plan, you'll find concrete tools for tapping your social skills, becoming a resource for others, and building a network that can help your business and profession—and your personal life.

Many of us already know why we need to network continually. Unfortunately, the word *networking* has been misunderstood and often has a negative impression because so many people are interested only in "What's in it for me?" and want quick results.

Instead, look at networking as a process of developing and maintaining quality relationships that enrich your life and empower you to achieve your goals. It's about giving first and realizing that we can learn from everyone we meet.

What you need is a step-by-step approach to networking effectively and methodically, to work it into your everyday life, no matter who you are or what you do. You also need to practice consistent networking and make it work in your life and lifestyle. One size does not fit all. Someone in a class once told me that networking is similar to flossing your teeth: If you fail to do it every day, you won't reap the benefits.

Network Like You Mean It: The Definitive Handbook for Business and Personal Networking focuses on how to increase your business and achieve your goals—by reaching out to people. It also explores how to network in your personal life and expand and enrich your circles. You'll soon see how both personal and business networking have many similarities.

You'll discover a system that's simple to remember and incorporate into your life, based on five practices:

1. Meet new people and nurture your current networks.

2. Listen and learn from everyone with whom you connect.

3. Make quality connections for others.

4. Follow up consistently.

5. Stay in touch creatively.

You'll see in these pages that networking is a lifelong process and a state of mind. The opposite of *networking* is *not working*. Ross, a client who's become a friend, told me that many business professionals understand how to provide their clients with excellent customer service during the "state of the transaction." The challenge is learning how to maintain and cultivate that same relationship—and more—in between transactions. This is building a relationship.

How do you distinguish yourself from others, move your business relationships to the next level, and also be time sensitive and efficient? One goal, as Ross told me, is to find a way to leverage relationships into "dynamic partnerships." Each part of finding, growing, and keeping business relationships weaves into another, and you need to have all three components to create really strong business and personal relationships that will help your business. Ask yourself these questions:

- Who am I? Am I an entrepreneur, part of a small or large company, a manager, or a salesperson?

- What are my goals, and how do I want to achieve them?

- What do I have to offer others?

- What can I give, and how can I be a resource?

- How do I market myself with my experience and expertise?

- Where and when will I do it?

This book is divided into three parts. In Part 1, "Find (Meeting People)," you'll discover how and where to find new connections, and you'll build your checklist for maximizing every event you attend. Part 2, "Grow (Building on Your Strengths)," shows you how to grow your relationships to their fullest potential. Part 3, "Keep (Maintaining Your Hard-Earned Relationships)," helps you keep your contacts, friends, clients, and all relationships coming back. Each chapter includes stories from my personal experience and from people like you who have shared their experiences. Each chapter also concludes with exercises you can do as you build on the skills you've learned, and you'll find an appendix of reference materials to consult for more.

You might be thinking, "Easy for her! She makes this all sound so simple—but I think this is hard!" I understand entirely—I'm an introvert. I've spent my life researching, learning, and developing the skills that now make me someone others many times perceive as an extrovert. At public events or when I'm connecting with someone individually, I often say that I'm a "learned extrovert." You, too, can use the strategies I offer in this book to personalize a plan that works to make you an effective networker.

You already have all the tools inside you—it's just a matter of developing a system and sticking to it.

PART 1

Find (Meeting People)

1

Who Do You Know?

"Everyone has a story to tell. Bring new people into your life. Everyone you meet is an opportunity to learn from, give to, and be a resource."
—Anonymous

On a trip to Kenya, you can imagine my surprise when Massai warrior Chief William asked for my card and then emailed me! Remember, the tribe lives without electricity. The chief walks 10 miles to the village daily and uses the computer at the store where he buys beads for his tribe to make jewelry. We've stayed in touch over the years, and he has created and developed a nonprofit foundation that reaches across East Africa.

In whatever you do, be sure to *get and retain* business *and/or a fulfilling position* and also find relationships that will continue throughout your life. In order to "find," you must have a strategy, plan, and tactics that you can implement for daily help. Some people might consider themselves the "hunters," or the ones who find new opportunities, but you also need to fine-tune your skills as you create new relationships and build and nurture the ones you have.

In the first section of this book, you tackle only those aspects involved in finding relationships and business opportunities—everything from meeting new people to identifying where and how you can do it easily and efficiently. You learn what to do at an event to make your time more efficient and productive as you're networking. I have also put together a model that you can modify according to your own needs and a strategic guide to help you in any business—or, for that matter, any life situation.

The opposite of networking is *not* working. Every day, I start out by thinking, "Who will I meet today?"

Sitting on an airplane one day awaiting takeoff, I looked around the cabin and realized that each person had his or her own story and many different networks. Any conversation could teach me something new or let me help the person I talked with.

I decided to experiment and noticed that the woman sitting across the aisle was reading a book on sales and marketing. When we were served our sodas and nuts, I asked her whether the book was interesting and mentioned that I hadn't read that one yet. We began our conversation, and I learned that she was a new sales manager for a software company and was on her way to a sales meeting in Los Angeles. Through some open-ended, conversational questions I asked, I learned the following:

- She lived in New York City, in the same building as a friend of mine, and they knew each other from their condo board.

- She formerly worked for a company where I had presented a workshop.

- She was an active alumni member of a university that a friend's daughter was interested in and said she would write a letter of recommendation to the admissions office after speaking with the young woman.

Through this exchange, I realized that, in business and in life, networking happens anywhere, anytime. You never know how starting a conversation with someone can open doors and opportunities for both parties involved. In a Woody Allen movie, I once heard the comment, "Life is networking"—and I agree.

The art of networking, which I define as the combination of people skills, interaction, and opportunity, is an absolutely vital tool for building business and keeping it. Networking is about creating and developing opportunities by meeting and connecting the dots among the people you know. Over time, as you build rapport and trust, these relationships lead to other contacts, relationships, and opportunities—and friendships develop. As you read this, I hope you are saying, "Of course! This is life and what I do daily—I just don't call it *networking*."

The power created by this amazing link of trusted advisers, friends, and advocates is stunning. Think of those you know who are truly masterful at networking, and ask yourself, "How do they do it? What do they do?" You'll find that their "best practices" vary greatly, but regardless of their communication and personality style, these people all have confidence and respect for each other.

Now think of all the networks you already have:

- Jobs (clients and colleagues)
- Social activities
- Religious affiliations
- Neighbors, friends, and relatives
- Clubs (social and business)
- Business and professional associations
- Social media
- Hobbies and interests
- School alumni

The list goes on and on.

I read years ago that we all know at least 250 people. Look at the group of people you know who fit in this list. You can multiply your network by helping many of these people, who can then connect you with some of the 250 people each of them knows. In my own life, this number has multiplied many times over!

By the way, I've stayed in touch with that woman from the plane. She was able to help my friend's daughter get into the university she wanted (of course, the young lady did have good grades and was both an athlete and an all-around terrific young lady, yet my new friend's influence helped), and I ended up doing an executive coaching project for her company. I also reconnected with her former company, which I had previously worked with. Just by taking some action steps, I was able to make more connections that led to other business opportunities that I'm nurturing today.

Here's one reason I hope you're reading this book: to learn to look at life with a networking eye and ear and realize that opportunities can unfold anywhere, anytime. You just have to be ready, willing, able, and open to starting some conversations. Be open to serendipity and the path to synchronicity. There are no accidents—everyone we connect with can be a resource or lead us to the next opportunity.

Write down the names of up to three people you know in each of the following categories:

Job/workplace: _____

                                  _____

                                  _____

Social activities: _____

                                  _____

                                  _____

Religious affiliations: _____

                                  _____

                                  _____

Neighbors/friends   _____

                                  _____

                                  _____

Clubs: _____

                                  _____

                                  _____

Professional associations: _____

                                  _____

                                  _____

School/alumni associations: _____

                                  _____

                                  _____

Now look over these names and recall how you met some of these people. How were you introduced? Did you introduce them to others? Perhaps you have to jog your memory a bit. The end result is that you'll realize that networking has been part of your life, even if you've never consciously thought about it.

Part of growing and strengthening your business networks is remembering who else was involved when you met and realizing that each of you probably does know more than 250 people. Let me share a few of my examples.

While sipping espresso at a coffee shop, I was talking with a friend about his advertising agency. Noticing that the man at the next table was listening, I introduced myself and asked if he was in advertising as well. He said he was, but he was currently looking for a job. I introduced the two men and later heard that the man at the next table got an interview at my friend's firm.

In another case, I was in an art class and complimented a woman on her bracelet. We began talking, and I ended up ordering the bracelet from her firm and attended an event held by the designer. Now she and I are working on a consulting project. All that came from admiring a piece of jewelry and following up.

As a third example, one afternoon, Bill, a successful realtor, received a call from a woman who left this message: "I am in Los Angeles at a hotel with my two kids, and I'm unemployed and need to find a house." He called her back and agreed to meet to see how he could help. This woman turned out to be the wife of the new coach of a major sports team, and they were relocating. Bill sold the family a great house and has gotten several more referrals from other team members. Following up made the difference: The woman had left the same message for five other brokers, none of which returned her call. When Bill told the initial part of the story to the other 90 agents in his office, they all remarked, "Waste of time." But who's laughing now?

These examples, and countless others, show that almost any person you come in contact with is a potential networking contact. Be aware, and develop new business opportunities when you're on an airplane, at the dentist's office, in line for movie tickets, and even at the dry cleaner.

People You Need in Your Network

The first step in building a network is to identify the people with whom you want to build relationships. You will be pleasantly surprised by how many of them you already know. The types of people you need in your network most likely include the following categories:

- Customers and clients
- Suppliers
- Coworkers and colleagues
- People in your profession
- People you went to school with or met at a seminar or workshop
- Like-minded people
- Neighbors
- Friends
- Family
- People you meet "in everyday life"

Customers or Clients

These people are the lifeblood of your business, and it is important to build positive relationships with them. The more you know about them, and the more they know about and trust you, the more both of you will prosper.

You might be thinking, "This category doesn't apply to me. I don't have customers or clients."

In my workshops, I often ask, "By a show of hands, how many of you are in sales? How many in customer service? How many in public relations? How many own and run a business? How many manage a team of employees?" Some hands go up.

Then I ask, "How many of you have to convince another person to use an idea of yours? How many of you are looking for a new job, a promotion, or a raise?" By the end of my questions, almost everyone has raised his or her hand. The fact is, we are all in sales, customer service, or public relations, regardless of our formal job description.

When you think about it, you are constantly communicating messages and selling your ideas to others. We are all public relations specialists when we act as representatives of our companies or ourselves. Your "clients" include coworkers, staff, other department heads, and, certainly, your boss. In fact, anyone you "sell" your thoughts or ideas to is a client.

If you are in sales, keeping customers happy and profitable members of your network is essential. Besides being the lifeblood of your current business, they can be your advocate by referring you to prospects, thereby helping your business to grow and prosper. And you can do the same for them. Many of us don't like the word *sales* and almost cringe at the thought of it. Let's look at it from the perspective of hotels such as the Ritz-Carlton or the Hilton, where everyone in the organization is part of the customer experience—let's think of it that we all work to create the best experience.

CREATING A POSITIVE EXPERIENCE

Use these networking tactics to keep those you connect with satisfied and happy.

- **Know them.** Find out their hobbies, names of family members, likes and dislikes, birthdays and anniversaries, and even their favorite foods. Keep good records of this information, and use it to build on your relationships.

- **Keep in touch.** Share information and ideas with customers when you think it will help them. Even if nothing develops, it will provide an opportunity to be on their radar screen. Remember, your goal is to make lasting impressions.

- **Handle complaints and concerns promptly.** Take responsibility for problems, no matter who caused them. Your customers will see you as their lifesaver and will want to help you in return.

- **Prove that you are dependable.** When you make promises, keep them! This builds trust, an important factor in any relationship.

We expand on this later as we move into keeping your relationships.

Suppliers

Whether you own a business or work in a company, you buy goods and services from suppliers or vendors. Think of all the products and services you buy in your business and in your personal life.

Your suppliers can be anyone. Other than your business contacts, they could include your dry cleaner, your hairdresser, and even your doctor. My IT tech, John Mazzaraco, once overheard me on the phone with someone as he was installing some software and said, "Andrea, I know the head of purchasing of the company you're calling." Turns out they were friends growing up. As you can imagine, having the referral from John was a huge help and got me through right away. I also returned a favor to him by introducing him to one of my strategic partner clients, and now he is doing that person's computer work. Remember, this is a two-way street. Over the years, we have exchanged many referrals and opportunities because of the trust we have in each other and feel comfortable referring each other.

Just as I was writing this book, my hairdresser, who knows the real color of my hair, was planning a surprise birthday cruise for his significant other. He asked me who I knew, and I was able to connect him with my new part-time neighbor in Florida, who lives in the same condo building and is a cruise specialist! Bingo—a true win/win on all fronts.

Again, 24/7 networking awareness helps everyone.

FUNNY THING IN THE DOCTOR'S OFFICE

As I walked into the office, my doctor came out front to meet me. I'm always impressed by how he greets each patient by name, no matter how full the waiting room is. As I walked back to the exam room, I passed his office. On his desk was the first book I had written.

I said to him a few minutes later, "Dr. S., you are good!" He looked at me curiously, and I explained. "Well, here I was visiting your office today, and you pulled out my book to put right on your desk. That's great, and it makes me feel important." He smiled and said, "Andrea, I've got to tell you, it's been there since you gave it to me! It's a great paperweight, and other people always pick it up and ask about it!"

Whether you've written a book or not, you can always give others something that will help keep your name in their mind. (He will now get a copy of this book!)

Coworkers and Colleagues

Look around your office and throughout your organization. Some people you know fairly well—they might even be your friends. For the others, you could set a goal to get to know them better. Start your action plan by asking them out for lunch or coffee, or volunteer on a task force so that you'll have more interaction with them. The fact is, the people who work with us and know us are a powerful source for networking.

Janice works in the legal department of a large organization. Through her relationships, she found a new apartment, got in touch with a new carpenter, and was able to help one of her friends at another company get a job at her organization. How? It all happened through the power of internal networking. She has also gotten into the habit of learning more about her colleagues and coworkers. Janice takes the time to learn about their interests. One day at lunch with a colleague, she discovered that her best friend's husband was the sales director of a company where her sister was interviewing. Her sister was very qualified, yet many other people were, too, and the interviewing process was tough. Thanks to the personal introduction, her sister got the "job of her dreams." That's just more evidence of how the concept "You just never know" applies here. We'll look into how to develop your internal business relationships across departments more later.

Yet too often I hear this: "In my company, we work in 'silos.' How can I strengthen my relationships with other departments?" This is a critical question because we're all working for the same bottom line, and each person with whom we interact is someone we can learn from and possibly cooperate with at work. Larger companies often find out too late that one department is working with a prospective client, and other departments could have added their expertise to help close the sale or move the business along. Sadly, no "crossover" discussion occurs, and business is lost because of it.

You and your coworkers form a "chain of value" that can reach more potential clients than your efforts working in isolation from each other. You are all internal invaluable resources for one other. You might ask yourself:

- What links do I have with other coworkers and departments?
- Do people know what I can do to help them? And do I know what they do?
- What are our common goals?
- Are we committed to learning from each other's ideas and creating new possibilities together?

One law firm that I consulted with realized that it could develop more business if the partners and associates learned more about each other's practice areas. In putting together a workshop for the firm, I asked the members what questions they had about their firm's other departments. Each attorney came to the program with a mission statement of what his or her department did and suggestions on how all of them could work more productively with other areas.

At the end of the program, each person was charged with staying in touch with someone from another practice area, to see what new opportunities could develop. The challenge after these events is always whether people will get out of their comfort zone and change. Most lawyers, like all professionals, are already overworked, yet this internal networking focused on the bottom line. Partners saw how they could gain new business. I'm happy to report that, after six months, this law firm developed two new pieces of business from the internal relationships they established.

A NETWORKING OPPORTUNITY FOR YOU

We can all do this. Think about your own internal teams. See where you can uncover new business opportunities right in your own backyard while also making everyone better team players.

Effective networking is often woven throughout the mission statements, core values, and career growth models of corporations:

- Provides access to key contacts to help you grow in your career

- Permits informational exchanges

- Leverages the knowledge and experience of others to understand what drives the firm's business

- Connects you to a wider array of people who can help educate you, and vice versa

STARTING A NEW JOB

Pete, a young man I have worked with, really goes out of his way to learn about people and their interests. When Pete took a new job, one of the first things he did was draw a map of his new office area, noting each cubicle and office. As he met people, he wrote down their names on the corresponding space on his map, along with interesting things he learned about them in conversation: the names of their children, their favorite vacation spots, any sports they play and other outside interests, and favorite restaurants, as well as work information. Pete created a foundation for strong business relationships with these people right from the start. From my last report with him, he has steadily moved up the ranks of his firm—and he credits much of it for his internal networking and alliance-building practices.

People in Your Business or Profession

I enjoy developing relationships with other people in my different businesses. Some people view this category of people as competitors, and in some ways we are—yet we can also refer, help, and leverage our relationships with each other. I know, for example, that often when I am called for a large project, I must bring in a team of consultants. Because I continually develop strong relationships with other subject matter experts, I always have a "team" of people waiting. They feel the same way, and sometimes I work with them as part of their virtual group. By removing our egos, we both make room for more new business.

I have developed contacts in companies that were not initially interested in my services. Yet because I was working with others in my business who already had relationships with those businesses, they came to see what I can do to help them. Carol is a perfect example. She also has a communications consulting firm and has hired me on several occasions to team up with her to conduct a part of a program in which I have expertise. Another time, I called on another executive coach friend to do a project for one of my clients. It all boils down to the fact that I trust these people, and I know their work. We have formed great strategic alliances. No person is an island, and we work better knowing that we have formed great networks.

You can do the same. Start to observe the people you know in your business and profession. They can become your network of advisers, and their connections will be helpful after you build a relationship with them.

Obvious places to meet people in your profession are on LinkedIn and in physical business meetings, conferences, association meetings, trade shows, meet-ups, and wherever people gather formally or informally to share ideas and news about your industry. As you become more successful in your profession, be sure to join professional associations and special-interest groups; attend seminars, workshops, and conventions; and become an active participant in these programs and groups.

Be willing to share your experience and expertise with those you are getting to know. Think of it this way: A fist tightly clenching what it has is unable to grab new opportunities. Be open to others, and you can receive from them. Such was the case with Margaret, a successful trainer and someone I have shared with generously. Because of our business relationship, she referred me to one of her clients to speak at a conference. Margaret knows my work, and she knew that I would honor her client relationship and be sure to keep her in the loop. We also have a business relationship and alliance. Want this technique to work for you? Find one professional contact whose business you'll offer to help grow. You'll see other opportunities emerge over time.

People You Went to School with or Met at a Workshop or Seminar

I'm involved with my college alumni organization and was asked to speak at one of its meetings. The contacts I reopened there led me to opportunities in two new industries, and I was asked to return to my former college campus to speak with the students. This came about because a former classmate of mine, now one of the managing directors of a large securities company, heard me speak at a conference and referred me to my college's business school. Take a closer look at your alumni e-zine or magazine, with an eye toward people who can help you or whom you can help in your profession. On LinkedIn, connect with those people and then follow your university or grad school. Make sure you also keep that college magazine abreast of your achievements for inclusion in the publication—you never know whom you might reconnect with. Again, the opportunities are limitless.

A colleague's niece, a recent graduate of a leading technical college, launched a successful career as a photographer's stylist in New York City based almost solely on contacts with alumni of her school. She actually knew very few of them before moving to New York City, yet she sought them out and found them willing to help her because they were fellow alumni. At a recent workshop, a young woman named Sarah mentioned, "Everything that has happened to me since college is a result of the people I met in classes and my sorority."

In another instance, a good friend had just landed a large project with the U.S. Air Force. I asked her how she'd been able to get connected, and she said, "Andrea, this goes back to a friend in my college sorority. Of course, it didn't happen overnight. We've been friends and always found ways to stay connected." Just for the record, my friend has been out of school for at least 25 years. It pays to stay in touch.

At one of my yoga classes, I always talk with Norma, who is in the public relations business, in between poses. Over time, she invited me to speak at an association lunch when the featured speaker canceled at the last minute. At that meeting, I connected with two people I have started to build professional relationships with—all because Norma and I shared conversations over time in yoga. Of course, I always keep her in the loop whenever an opportunity comes up as a result of her help. This is *key*: Always keep your initial introduction sources in the loop on any referral or introduction, whether they come together or not.

Meeting Ross is an example of giving and getting much in return. He sat in the front row of a seminar where I donate my time for a nonprofit professional association. After the program, he sent me a note, and we stayed in touch. (Talk about a wonderful note writer! Ross wins the award: He regularly sends me cards and articles of interest.) After about a year, I was invited in to work with Ross's team at one of his company's sales meetings. I got to help Ross, too—as I was getting my real estate license, I ran into someone he used to work with and reconnected them.

YOU ALREADY HAVE A MUCH LARGER NETWORK THAN YOU THINK

Curious about how big your current network might be? Find out by answering these questions:

- How many people do you work with now?

- How many people have you worked with in the past?

- How many clients or customers do you have, both past and present?

- How many people do you know from professional organizations?

- How many people do you know from other organizations, such as health clubs, your homeowners' association, or your children's school groups?

- How many people do you know from your religious affiliations or organizations?

- How many professionals (doctors, lawyers, accountants, and so on) do you come in contact with?

- How many former schoolmates do you stay in touch with?

- How many people do you know in your neighborhood?

- How many friends and relatives do you have?

Add them up. Chances are, you already have a large network of contacts.

Like-Minded People

Often the easiest people to talk with are those who have common interests and ambitions, or who share similar life experiences. And not just professionally—after all, you have a personal life, and that's a huge part of our networking! Think language classes, charity groups, kids' soccer games and recitals, vacations, and religious groups. The people you find at these events and places like the same things you do, and that leads to a perfect networking opportunity. You form your own niches when you start hanging out and meeting with people who share a passion or interest.

I like to collect jewelry. It's something I inherited from my wonderful mother, and I know she's smiling down at me from heaven. You might wonder what this has to do with my business. Well, one day, one of my former clients asked me to have breakfast with him and his friend, Dan, who had been the publisher of a jewelry magazine and was now looking for another position. We had an interesting meeting, and because I was engrossed in the subject matter of the jewelry industry, I was able to give him some leads. He eventually landed the top position at one of the leading jewelry publications through one of the connections I'd introduced him to. I was thrilled. It feels good to connect and help great people when the opportunities arise—and they often do. Just live life with that 24/7 networking awareness.

It just so happened Dan's editorial offices were in Bangkok, and I was going to be visiting there. Dan put me in touch with the chief editor, Robert, and I was able to become a contributor and write articles for the publication on developing new business. As I wrote for them on the very topics we are discussing here—how to find, grow, and keep your business—I had a great deal of fun: After all, I was doing it for an industry that I'm personally interested in. And you never know who will read the articles. How can you do the same with an industry that you are interested in expanding into more?

What do you really enjoy, and how can you start to create new connections for business in that area? Find ways to be visible. For example, you could write an article or make a presentation on your area of expertise at a business function where potential clients will be.

Neighbors

Neighbors can serendipitously become valuable members of your network. One small independent publisher of children's books has found several of her best authors in the small town where she lives. Most of us could get to know our neighbors better. Too often we just wave as they drive by, or we chat about our gardens, traffic, or the weather. Living in New York City, sometimes I see people only in the mailroom or elevator. I decided to change that and, over the years, have gotten to know quite a few people—not only in my building, but also in a two-block radius.

Start an experiment to take relationships with your neighbors to a new level. Go beyond the back-fence or mailroom conversations, and really get to know them by using some of the techniques you'd use at a business networking event. You might be surprised to find a neighbor in the same business, or a related one, or one who knows someone you want to meet. Of course, good neighbors are always an invaluable source for such things as cleaning services, contractors, organizations, decorators, or, when the time comes to move or expand, real estate agents. If you're reading this and thinking, "I need some down time," I understand— take the best and leave the rest! I'm just reinforcing that the potential of meeting new people has no limit. Operate within your pace and style— this is not a race.

NETWORKING IN YOUR ELEVATOR

John always said hello to a certain man in the elevator of his building. The man always nodded and asked how John's dad was doing. One day they started talking. John learned that the man, Tom, was the publisher of one of his favorite publications. John confided that he worked in the advertising business but was not in a position he particularly enjoyed. The two men stayed in touch, always saying hello when they met. Then one day Tom mentioned that he had an opening on his staff and asked John to send his resume. "I ended up working for 14 of the best years of my life for the man in the elevator," says John. The two became close friends, and when Tom passed away, his wife asked John to give the eulogy at his memorial—and specifically requested that he tell the elevator story as part of his "Tales with Tom."

Along the same lines, I know someone in Chicago who routinely strikes up conversations in the elevator. When he meets someone new in his office building, he looks at the button the person pushed and says, "Hi, my name is Bill. May I ask what kind of business you are in on the seventh floor?" He makes great new connections in less than 30 seconds.

Friends

Friends make the world a happier place. We need to welcome and nurture these people in our lives, as well as consider them important members of our network. What better advocate can we have, or can we be, than a friend? Take time to nurture and cultivate your friends. Network with them in a positive way, never with expectations. Give without the thought of receiving or keeping score, and you will receive the greatest gift of all: a good friend. When something more comes of it, consider that a gift.

My friend Bill, who works in the financial services industries, is one of those people who always looks for ways to help his friends. He gives freely of himself and receives introductions all the time. Why? Because he stays on all his friends' radar screens; when someone needs a financial adviser or is looking for help, he immediately comes to mind. I know that I look for ways to introduce him to others and keep an eye out for opportunities that would be good for his business. I also trust him and admire Bill's knowledge of his field and the pride he takes in his work. I know that he would do a great job in any project he undertakes.

How do you find the time to see your friends? Make plans to meet for breakfast, lunch, or dinner. Even better, look for unusual activities to share. I have met friends for walks (the new "in" for meetings and health benefits at the same time), afternoon tea, shopping excursions, workouts at the gym (chatting on the treadmill or bike is also good for your heart), and art lectures. Go to a sports event; play golf, tennis, or any other sport; or have a drink together after work. Take the time to do these things for your friends and for your own enrichment.

Family

Network with your family? When you know them well and believe in them and their work and ambitions, creating connections is easy. A friend of mine recently told me she recommended her nephew, a graphic artist, for a project for her company. She was familiar with his work and was confident he could do a quality job, quote a reasonable price, and meet the deadlines. Remember, her reputation was at stake, as it would have been with any recommendation she made. She also wisely distanced herself from the financial negotiations. Both she and her nephew were very clear with one another that this was a business arrangement and that, no matter the outcome, it would remain so. In this case, it worked out just fine. He did a good job, as she knew he would, and has received several subsequent assignments.

Networking with your family can work. Just be sure to maintain your integrity and be mindful of the reputations involved.

I'm always looking for opportunities to refer my dentist, Dr. Allan Miller, who is also my cousin. He has been my dentist my whole adult life. At a cocktail party last year, a couple mentioned that they lived in the same community as Dr. Miller, and I asked if they'd heard of him. The wife already is a patient, and the husband was impressed because Dr. Miller had referred him to an excellent specialist for work my cousin doesn't do. Again, this is networking and building connections at its finest.

People You Meet by Chance or in the Serendipity of Life

This is where the fun starts. These people seem to come into your life by chance and from almost anyplace: on planes and trains, at the grocery store, at Starbucks or Dunkin' Donuts, or wherever you happen to be. To make these chance encounters work for you, treat those you meet as important people to have in your network. Keep your ears and eyes open for these opportunities through chance encounters.

While visiting a friend in the hospital in Florida, I was sitting in the waiting room and started talking with the woman next to me. I was fascinated by her time management and organizational skills, even in the hospital waiting room.

As we talked, I learned about her business and the types of clients she worked with. By the time I was allowed into my friend's room, I had made a new contact and had already referred her to two new business projects. And from her, I learned many new tips and tricks on being better organized than I already was. We can always learn something new from someone when we are open to it.

One time in a New York taxi on my way to a dinner party, I started chatting with the driver, who told me that he loved the people of New York because they were so helpful. I learned during our 10-block ride (you might know about New York City traffic) that he was a lawyer from another country. When he'd moved to the United States, he'd had to start over in law school, all while he was working as a paralegal and driving a cab to support his family. Talk about determination! I gave him my card and asked him to email me his resume to see if I could do anything to help. I first wanted to see if he would follow up and whether he was for real. Well, he did—and he does have the credentials. I have already sent his information to two people. You never know what will happen, yet I'm sure my driver, Sangiv, will find some wonderful opportunities. I'm so glad that I was in his cab and, as always, had on my networking eyes and ears. You just never know!

Keep your eyes and ears open—serendipitous opportunities happen all the time, anywhere. This can happen when you log in to Twitter, Facebook, or LinkedIn and answer a message in a group question; when you comment on a picture; or when you reply to a tweet. Be open to the opportunities that develop.

Virtually everywhere is open ground. Those who might still think that networking is *getting* may think this seems like too much. Separate yourself from that mindset by remembering the most important aspect of networking: that it's about being open and willing to help and *give* first. Just make a connection. You might have heard that people come into our lives for a reason, a season, or a lifetime, and often we don't know which they fall into. Over time, we realize it.

Resist being cynical—concentrate only on the good things that happen when you surround yourself with positive thoughts and vibes.

Reconnect with People You Already Know

Make a game plan for reconnecting with the people who are already in your network. Start with a list of people in each of the categories we've just discussed, and add a few others that come to your mind who will accept your phone call, email, text, or social media invitation. Now reach out to them to touch base, say hello, or catch up on what has been happening in your lives. With all our technology tools and engines, we all know this is a daily "to do" and a common way people connect—and, more importantly, reconnect.

This happened to me recently. I received two emails from people from my "history." Both had read an article in which I was quoted, along with several others, and they'd gone to my website and reached out. One person had been the president of the company where I'd worked in my first sales job. Although I knew him somewhat, all these many years later, it was so nice to hear from him. I might even do a consulting project for his firm. (If not, it's still a great reconnection.) The other person was a woman who had worked for me when I was the publisher of a magazine. She called to say how excited she was to reconnect. We caught up, and I found out that she has her own business. I've already sent some people to her store in Minnesota.

I also recently reconnected with someone from my past as I was doing research on LinkedIn. I found a fantastic subject matter expert who is one of the top gurus in listening, Dr. Manny Steil. He'd spoken at my first sales meeting when I was starting out in advertising sales. I'd been so impressed with Dr. Steil and always remembered how he left an indelible print in my mind on the power of superior listening skills (something we work on daily). We reconnected and are now talking, and I've referred him and his book to many others. What a wonderful reconnection for me!

When you make that first reconnect, instead of feeling awkward, keep in mind the positive impact. The person might have been thinking of you and meaning to reach out, yet life got in the way. This has happened to me countless times. These reach-outs are easy to make because you're not going to be asking for anything. Be prepared. If you've been out of touch for a while, the person might respond cordially, yet you know he or she is thinking, "What do you want?" Imagine the person's surprise and pleasure when this turns out to be purely a friendly catch-up. Perhaps you are reaching out to congratulate him or her on something. LinkedIn gives us this opportunity daily.

FOUR-MULA FOR SUCCESS

Connect with four people per week from your universal database, including people from these categories:

1. A client or prospect with whom you have not been in touch for a while

2. A former business colleague

3. A friend you haven't been in touch with recently

4. A current friend

The final connect, to a current friend, will be the easiest and most fun— think of it as a reward for making the other three. This is a great way to keep nurturing our friendships—they're part of our network, and they also want us to be happy, just as we want the same for them. It's a win/win always. And no matter how well we know someone, we don't know everyone he or she knows. So many times, I've found mutual connections that we never initially realized. As you work through your list, you will find that many past relationships have become current ones. Keep it going. It's easy to fit four connects a week into your busy schedule. It breaks down the formidable task of reconnecting with your contacts into manageable, bite-size tasks—baby steps, as I like to call it. Make it a practice you continue as your network grows. Most important will be the results. Imagine, once you've solidified your relationship, how simple it will be to ask later if you ever need a favor.

Identify Key Business Contacts You Would Like to Meet

Make a list of key people in your industry or profession that you'd like to meet. Make them specific individuals (or specific titles of individuals, if you don't know the name of the current person in that position) within an organization or industry group who would be beneficial to your career or business goals. Aim high! Include high-level executives and high-profile people in your field. Again, LinkedIn makes this simple to navigate.

With LinkedIn or any search engine, do your research and determine organizations, interest groups, or places you could meet these people. Think about people they know, people you know, and the possible connections that might lead to a meeting. No connection is impossible.

One new woman in my network, Karen, owns a graphic arts company. She and I met on the chance that we might have opportunities to work with one another or people each of us knew.

I liked Karen's style, and I sent four letters of introduction to some of my clients for her. She, in turn, wrote a great letter of introduction to a company that I have always wanted to work with and that she already has as a client. When I sent my initial email, I connected right away, and the process of working with the organization is steadily underway. I knew this company and the person I wanted to talk with, yet I didn't have a connection until Karen referred me to someone who could start the process.

You can see how we have all sorts of people in our network without even realizing it. We have also looked at whom you need to get to know to strengthen your universal network. In the next chapter, you'll be getting ready to step out to the places where you'll get to network with current and new contacts. Before you attend your next meeting, take some time to look into your current network with the following exercise—it will lay a foundation for many opportunities in the future.

Exercise: Who's in Your Current Network?

This exercise is designed to help you bring to mind the people in your current network. When you think long enough about the people you've connected with throughout your life, you'll realize that you're in a much better position than you might have originally thought.

Your Immediate Network

This network includes people who would quickly answer or return a call, email, or text from you. For each type of person listed, name up to three people you would consider as part of your immediate network.

Customers of clients

1.

2.

3.

People from whom you buy products or services

1.

2.

3.

Coworkers

1.

2.

3.

Professional colleagues

    1.

    2.

    3.

Friends and neighbors

    1.

    2.

    3.

People in Your Secondary Network

Your secondary network includes people you connect with periodically. They might include people you went to school with, people you worked with at a previous job, friends from an old neighborhood, or people you met by chance and have found interests in common with. List up to five people in this category; beside each name, note how you met the person.

    1.

    2.

    3.

    4.

    5.

People in Your Universal Network

If you had to create an Excel spreadsheet of everyone you know, how many people would be on it? Chances are it would be a much longer list than the names you just listed in your immediate and secondary networks. This long list of your universal network is something to go back to every few months, to see what has changed in your business life that warrants getting in touch. Say you have several medical industry contacts you haven't worked with for years. Right now they could be part of your universal network. If you change jobs, however, and start working with medical products, these people would move to your secondary or immediate network. Your network is a living database that you need to nurture and maintain.

Networking Ladder

- **Top rung:** Your immediate network—people who connect via any form of communication from you right away

- **Middle rung:** Your secondary network—people who know who you are when you contact them

- **Lower rung:** Entire list of everyone you have ever known

Take-Away Reminders

Key exercise point: Check this list every three months to make sure you keep your network current. That way, you'll always have a list of people to reach out to when you're looking for a new opportunity or have something to help someone in your network.

Accountability: After each chapter, review and highlight the specific action steps you will take and how you will personally measure and monitor them.

In the Part 1 Appendix, you'll find a strategic networking guide that will help you with your action plans.

> *"Networking is the tool to open up doors. If you don't network, then get used to looking at a closed door."*
>
> —Jeri Sedlar, writer and coach

2

Where to Meet People

On my way to an adventure travelers' lecture, I stopped off to get a cup of tea. I started talking with a man in line who had a bag with the logo "World Traveler." I asked him his favorite country, and as we talked, I found out that he was the lecturer that evening for my travel class. I got to know John and have taken several of his tours around the world.

Today you have so many opportunities to meet new people both on- and offline. In this chapter, we focus on meeting and connecting face to face. Later we will look into the vast opportunities of meeting people online.

Where do people you want to know gather? Identify the different kinds of places, events, associations, trade organizations, and conferences where people in your profession, or the professions you are interested in, meet. Think about your potential and current clients and advocates—where do they go to connect? These are the types of locations where people get together to exchange and share information, contacts, and knowledge, as well as to purely enjoy each other's company.

Start building your list. What do you already know about these organizations? Do you belong to them and attend meetings? If so, how can you get more out of the organization and become more involved? Would you like to know more about these organizations and their members to find others who can help you build your network?

When you need to start a list from scratch, think first about your own professional and personal interests and passions. Do you go to your kids' parent–teacher meetings, watch their swim meets, or lead their scout troop? Do you belong to your neighborhood association or local historic group, sing in the choir at your church or synagogue, or work out at a local health club? Do you like to travel? Do you volunteer or contribute to charities? Do you belong to a book or financial club? Do you take dance, art, or language classes, or do you have any other hobby that you have a strong interest in? Thinking that conferences, meet-ups, and business meetings are the only places to go is too limiting. Most of us can think of how we started up a lifelong friendship or a business partnership from a chance meeting far outside a business environment. That's why I always say life is networking and serendipitous opportunities are everywhere. We just need to have what I call a 24/7 networking awareness.

Events and Organizations

You can meet potential business contacts at all different types of events. The first that comes to mind is the structured event whose stated purpose is to actively network and learn from each other. These can take place at associations and industry-specific group events, as well as at meetings of networking organizations. People who attend these events expect to introduce themselves and briefly discuss their business, in hopes of making a helpful business connection. In some ways, it's easier to go through the process of "active" networking at these events because that's their stated purpose. As you know, it takes time to make connections that stick and turn them into opportunities for both sides. Sadly, some people think that they simply need to show up a few times. But these types of events are the perfect place to start learning a little about the people you'd like to connect and start the process with. These exchanges can start the process of building trust, and people do business with those they trust and like. This accomplishes two goals: You find out whether you want to join the organization, and you expand your network by two.

Another opportunity to meet and make connections is at association and professional industry events. Here the stated purpose is either to conduct business or to address a specific topic of interest to the group. This is also a perfect opportunity to network and connect with other like-minded people. These events are great venues for creating the opportunities to make solid connections.

Industry organizations also hold social and cultural events either specifically to raise funds for a charity or to recognize industry leaders. As we all know, when you get involved in any group, there are often several opportunities to pursue. The key is to find the right group (or groups) where you can make a difference during the time you spend there and with those you connect with. The process is to get involved, attend meetings, and build relationships. The next sections describe some types of groups you might want to consider.

Associations and Industry-Specific Organizations

I grew up in the advertising and direct marketing industry. Like any industry, it has many different forums, councils, and meetings. Plenty of contacts, relationships, and business opportunities are developed at these events, all the result of active networking. You simply need to keep your eyes and ears open and have a process to follow (more on this when we discuss your networking checklist for every event you attend).

Often the stated mission of these organizations is educational, informational, or, for some trade associations, to review industry trends to identify any future opportunities. Most organizations are open to those who work in, or aspire to work in, the industry or profession they represent. I think of how many organizations I've found online and how much I've learned about social media by getting involved and attending different educational forums. I've met people who have helped me, and vice versa, and those who have become friends, vendors, and clients. All of these organizations provide a wide variety of services to members, including the opportunity to meet and connect with like-minded people. Becoming involved gives you the opportunity to meet people with whom you will feel a rapport and possibly build a relationship.

I have been involved and active in several organizations over the years that have helped me in my business. Two that have worked for me are the Financial Women's Association and Advertising Women of New York. Through the years, I have found clients, suppliers, friends, and mentors through these groups. I did not join them specifically because they are women's organizations; I joined them because they represented two industries I work in and wanted to learn more about. After I did my research and attended some meetings, both of these organizations kept coming to the top of my list.

Although I have reaped many rewards from these associations, I believe joining an organization is foremost about *giving*. Getting involved in committees, participating in webinars and workshops, and helping others along the way opened many doors for me. I always know that what gets remembered gets rewarded. The "it's a small world" effect holds true here. Countless people I've met at these associations have connected me to businesspeople I never would have met on my own. My secret? I do what you should do:

Take the time to get involved instead of just being a spectator.

You can find these groups and industry associations by asking others in your business or profession, or by reading online trade magazines and going to LinkedIn and joining different groups. Do an Internet search for organizations you know about, and also search with keywords to find others. When you find a group you think you'll like, be sure to check out its links and resources page. You'll likely be overwhelmed with the content and links to other organizations in the industries you have an interest in. Most organizations have a local chapter in your community, and you'll find everything on their home page. You can also visit the home page of the Center for Association Leadership (ASAE), www.asaecenter.org.

Joining and becoming active in one or several of these groups will provide you with many profitable networking opportunities and give your career a boost.

Networking Organizations

These are groups whose primary stated purpose is to network, build relationships, and exchange leads, contacts, and tips. Instead of being industry specific, they have members in different fields, yet with collaborative and partnership opportunities to grow your business opportunities. Search for any type of group you are interested in—business, hobby, special interest, cause that you support—and you will find organizations to choose from; simply decide what is the best use of your time, energy, and money.

Many groups are national in scope, with local chapters, so visit a couple meetings and employ the 2-2-2 strategy (see the "My 2-2-2 Strategy" sidebar in this chapter). Meeting schedules vary greatly, and with the mobile way we work today, you can find the right venue for you. Many organizations allow some or all attendees to give a brief elevator introduction (we talk more about preparing yours for this situation in Chapter 3, "Techniques for a Successful Networking Event"). With your networking checklist (discussed later and found in the appendix), you will be armed and totally ready to go.

Some networking organizations keep their members accountable. They keep track of who is actively receiving and giving leads to other members—and your membership often depends on being a giver first. Again, I look at many of these types of organizations as creating your own advisory board for business: You learn about others, and they learn about you. The end result is that you want to refer opportunities to them. What results can you expect? It depends on how much you and other members of your group are willing to contribute. If I had to offer a formula, it would be this:

Networking organization you like

+

Frequent attendance

+

Giving more than you receive

+

Following up with new contacts

+

Reporting back to the person who gave you the referral

=

Networking success

The best thing about these groups is that they are structured, have a facilitator, and keep the meeting on point with an agenda. This format seems to work well for many people, especially those of us who are introverted or uncomfortable with the activity of networking or asking for referrals. You can be great at your particular profession yet not be comfortable with this way of building your business. Let me show you how one of these groups works.

Several years ago, I was asked to be a luncheon speaker for the Executives' Association of New York (www.eanyc.com). I walked into a room of 85 people, all owners or principals of midsize businesses who come together weekly to share information, offer leads, and help with each other's businesses. They were excellent networkers and relationship builders, and here I was speaking to this group! Reading the audience, I quickly adapted my remarks to show how they could help coach their staffs to network and find new opportunities. As a result, they invited me to become their official "networking guru." This group operates like a business and has a clear business model for its members. Some of the members have been together more than 20 years, and the organization is international. I have made great connections and gotten some terrific and trustworthy vendors from the group, including my caterer, my travel agent, and even a business coach that I have also referred to many.

The system truly works. It's built on hardworking professionals, all experts in their fields, who come together to learn from and do business with their colleagues. Many wonderful friendships have also formed over the years.

Other types of networking groups you find might focus on job hunting. These are invaluable resources for networking and offer helpful tips and opportunities. The groups host meetings for networking, publish e-zines, and provide workshops and webinars to aid in job searches. In many cases, the group's website alone is an invaluable resource. A quick search on the Internet will yield similar sites, many of which are specific to your industry and interests.

Internal (Company) Meetings and Events

An important yet often overlooked opportunity for meeting and developing contacts is the internal business meeting or social event within your company. Recognizing the value of employees' internal networking, one company I know invited me to present at its annual meeting. We started off with an exercise that has since become a tradition for the group. The firm's employees start the first evening of their sales conference with this assignment. Each person is to find someone at the opening cocktail party event that he or she doesn't know well and learn something new about the person. Often the participants have already done an internal online search and visited each other's LinkedIn profiles. This builds a foundation for forming new alliances and contacts. The company has found that this simple exercise helps its associates work well together throughout the conference, as well as later when they return to their home offices. It also improves interactions with senior staff members. Our technology makes so much of this easy, possible, and fabulous!

All organizations have internal meetings, which are necessary for conducting business and continuing the lines of global communication. Companies also recognize the importance of making these opportunities internal networking environments: They seek to create and build internal alliances and develop more opportunities. One corporate program I delivered for 500 employees, from different departments and at all job levels, was titled *Building Your Internal Alliances and Advocates*. I approached the assignment with the strategy that, for the most part, this was a diversified group with a shared interest in the company's goals and mission. I was able to discuss the opportunities and advantages of meeting and developing associations with people across the firm, regardless of their position or title. To facilitate this, I incorporated tips and techniques for a successful event, such as creating a networking checklist (discussed in Chapter 3).

Many of us do this type of training on- or offline with professional services firms and corporations where people tend to work in what are sometimes referred to as "silos." We may rarely think of the resources available to us in other parts of their firm. The great reward is the feedback I get from people who mention that, as a result of some of the tools we discussed, they were able to connect and get to know someone in another department who has subsequently helped them in their work—and enabled them to help others as well.

An exercise that often works well for a regional or national company meeting is to have everyone drop his or her business card into a bowl. When people leave the meeting, they take out a card. Their assignment is to communicate with that person electronically. They need to introduce themselves, ask about the other person's goal from the meeting or session, set a follow-up date, and then actually speak for a few minutes to show some accountability. When the system works correctly, two connections are made: You make one, and someone else connects with you. This is a great way to start some internal team building, learn from each other, and make each meeting count. Try this in your own organization or department, and see what types of new connections and collaborations are made. In Chapter 3, we talk about finding out people's preferred method of communication. In this initial case, I find that people often email or text first and then follow up with a "live" conversation.

WAYS THAT I CAN HELP OTHERS

- Introduce and make connections for others

- Recommend products and services that have benefited me

- Share information I have learned

- Learn about other people's business so I can refer them

- Send them items of interest through multiple channels of communications

---

Everywhere Else...

Finally, there is everywhere else. Industry-related classes, seminars, and workshops where you go to further your skills are prime networking opportunities. Doing volunteer work or joining a neighborhood association or the board of your church or synagogue also provides opportunities to meet people you need in your universal network. However, avoid at all costs joining any group just to seek quick results. It won't happen. Follow your interests first. Enjoy yourself, learn a new skill, make a contribution, and meet and develop new contacts while you're at it.

I've included some ideas for you here, depending on your interests. You'll find a full guide in this book, with strategies and tips that will help you network and connect for any type of group you find yourself in. (Refer to the Part 1 Appendix.)

Service Groups

The mission of most nonprofit service organizations is to serve humanity. Members come from various walks of life and a variety of professions, so consider this another opportunity to build your network. Some organizations include these:

- Rotary clubs (I have had the great fortune to speak and attend chapters all over the world.)
- Chambers of commerce
- Political clubs
- League of Women Voters
- Charitable and fund-raising groups
- Museum and art leagues
- Religious groups
- Parent–teacher associations
- Homeowners' associations

The following are some of the largest organizations that provide service to those in need:

- Lutheran Services in America
- YMCA
- Salvation Army
- United Jewish Communities
- American Red Cross
- Catholic Charities USA
- Goodwill Industries International
- Boys & Girls Clubs of America

Whether you belong to any of these and leverage them as a networking resource depends on your interests and your inclination to volunteer your time and expertise to your community. These groups exist to serve the community; meeting and connecting with people is the bonus. As I have said, like-minded people are the people you want in your network; you will find these people at these organizations. In addition, at many charitable and fund-raising events, you will find executives and other business leaders who volunteer their time. What better way to get to know them, and for them to get to know your abilities, than to work together on such an event? Join, volunteer, and profit from these organizations.

MAKING AN INTEREST PAY OFF

For a great example of making an interest pay off, consider the case of a real estate agent I worked with on an article for the Women's Council of Realtors. She's also actively involved on the March of Dimes board in her community and in her church. Being part of these local groups has helped her build credibility in her community—and has also helped her real estate business. When people see that you're part of the community and a contributor to its welfare, they begin to trust you. You will become known to them as "the go-to expert" in your area of work, and people will start coming to you for your advice when the need arises. This can lead to business opportunities with them or recommendations to their friends and colleagues. Remember, you join these groups because you are sincerely interested and believe in them. However, you're always willing to give friendly advice or offer your services to those you know you can help.

Special-Interest Groups and Activities

Networking opportunities are everywhere—at your gym or yoga class, book club, chess club, salsa dance class, round-robin racquetball game, Wednesday evening church fellowship group, and exotic vacation destination of your choice. All of these groups are personally rewarding, but they can also help you make connections with like-minded people who could become valuable members of your network. I recall a friend worrying about an organized tour of Europe she was about to embark on: "What if I don't like any of the people I meet?"

"You will like them," I replied. "They enjoy the same things you do, or they would have chosen another tour."

I was right. She had a great time and came back with not only new friends, but also a number of professional contacts that subsequently benefited her business.

It's Not Just About the Event—Get Involved

By now, you have perceived that, to grow your network, you have to do more than join and attend. You have to get involved to meet new people and make a name for yourself. Here's my three-step process for involving yourself in any organization where you've identified people you'd like to know:

1. Go to meetings, meet people, and then *join* the organizations that best suit you.

2. Volunteer, join a committee, and *become active.*

3. Write an article, give a speech, and *become known.*

Go to Meetings, Meet People, and Join the Organizations That Best Suit You

As I've said before, if you're going to invest time and energy in an organization, make sure it's the best one for you. Most organizations encourage a prospective member to attend a couple meetings before joining. I highly recommend this, no matter what you think you already know about the organization. Use your networking techniques, and set a goal to meet at least two new people at each meeting you attend. Then set up a follow-up meeting with each person you met, to get to know him or her and find out more about the organization.

You'll discover from their answers whether future meetings will help you achieve your reasons for joining the organization. Yes, it's true that you always need to be open to connecting with people. However, you also have to make the most of your resources, your time, and money.

Research online the organization's past and upcoming meetings and events. Are these of interest and benefit to you? Are the speakers people you want to hear and meet? Are other programs and workshops offered that would help you in your profession? Read the group's newsletter and online materials. Read and rate its website. Is it useful and informative? Would you have something to contribute to a newsletter or a program? Start making your notes.

For each group or activity you consider, ask yourself:

- Who attends meetings and actively participates?

- Are these the people I want in my network?

- Is the group network friendly, willing to give and share information with others?

- Are the meetings, speakers, and activities of interest and benefit to me?

- What can I contribute that will be of interest and helpful to the group and its members?

When you feel satisfied with the answers to these questions, sign up. Join and become an active member.

MY 2-2-2 STRATEGY

Before you decide to join a group, apply this strategy:

- Attend two meetings.

- Meet two people and exchange business cards.

- Arrange two follow-up meetings for breakfast, lunch, or coffee.

This achieves two goals: You find out whether you want to join the organization, and you expand your network by two.

Volunteer, Join a Committee, and Become Active

Connecting with like-minded people is one of the reasons you join an organization. Becoming actively involved in what the organization does helps make you visible and get known.

Join the program committee, for instance, one of the most interesting and profitable committees in any organization. As an active member of this committee, you'll meet and interact with all the speakers and presenters—the experts in their field. Who in your industry would you like to meet yet have no logical way to do so? Perhaps you will be able to invite him or her to give a speech for your organization, and you will start to be on that person's radar screen.

If the program committee doesn't seem right for you, join another one that interests you. You will meet and get to know more people in a shorter time, and they will get to know you. When you only attend meetings, you limit your ability to really connect with other members. After all, the majority of the time spent at a meeting is devoted to the program, which usually involves listening to a speaker. And remember to take great notes and always find a reason to send a thank you note (either electronically or handwritten), to thank the speaker for his or her remarks and tell what you learned. You'll differentiate yourself and, over time, add new people to your network.

Or maybe you want to volunteer for the greeting and welcoming committee. The greeter meets everyone who attends the meeting, so you're guaranteed a chance to introduce yourself to everyone. Then you'll have an opening line to connect with them again later in the meeting. I love to do this, and it's a sure way to meet people. Also, for someone like me who can be introverted, it's a great icebreaker.

Become active in the organizations you join. Doing so will expand your network quickly and efficiently.

Write an Article, Give a Speech, and Become Known

One of the best ways to get your name in front of the members of an organization is to get your name in print. Remember how you checked out the organization's newsletter and website before you joined to see whether you could make a contribution? Now you know about the types of articles published in the newsletter or on the website, and it's time to make that contribution. Write an article and submit it to the editor or webmaster. Even if your article is just a recap of the last meeting, do it, get a byline, and get it published. You will start to gain name recognition—and, as I say, "Repetition causes recognition." Meeting people will be much easier when they remember your article and your professional credentials, which that article mentioned. In addition, you will be making a valued contribution to the organization and its members.

Giving a speech or presentation to your organization is another way to become known and meet more people. Organizations are always looking for program ideas or breakout sessions for larger meetings or conventions. Show them your expertise, and seize the opportunity to become a presenter on a topic you think could be beneficial to the group. If you fear public speaking (we all work at this throughout our lives), take a course in presentation skills and practice what you've learned whenever you have an opportunity. The ability to speak in front of a group is a necessary skill in the business world, even if it's a tough one for many of us. I've been teaching presentation skills for more than 20 years to hundreds of clients and thousands of participants, and I can assure you that learning and practicing these skills greatly boosts confidence and ensures success. I practice every single day. Offer to do a webinar or online video—let people see your expertise and passion.

Now that you know most of the places to find people (some tips and suggestions for online networking are found in Chapter 8, "The Introvert's Networking Advantage: The Quiet Way to Success"), you're ready to network in the traditional sense: at a structured event. The next chapter gives you a detailed checklist of what to do when it's time to network.

TEACH A CLASS

Giving a speech or presentation can be as simple as teaching a class on a topic you know. In addition to speaking and teaching in corporations, I keep myself fresh with the courses I teach at universities around the country. My participants have come from many different professions and industries. For example, last year my classes included a store owner, an attorney from a major firm, the owner of a midsize advertising agency, an intern at a large public relations firm, a seasoned orthodontist, an international banker, and a digital marketer, to name a few. It was wonderful to see these people making connections among themselves. In this class, as in so many others I've taught, I've made friends and business connections; my network continues to expand.

Developing a Niche as You Network

When you create a niche, you separate and differentiate yourself from others. You become the go-to person in your business for your specialty or expertise. As you network within a particular niche, you gain three main benefits: credibility, visibility, and differentiation.

Ask yourself some questions as you develop this area:

- What are my strongest interests?

- What makes me excited about a specific hobby, charity, or special interest?

- How do I like to spend my time when I'm not at work or with my family?

- What are my talents?

- How do I differentiate myself from others who also share my interest or passion?

Consider some ways to get started:

- Look at your existing list of connections and contacts, and identify the ones you enjoy spending the most time with and those who leave you feeling energized and valued.

- Determine common characteristics, and look at demographics, personality traits, and interests. Look at what solutions you provide for your clients and how your experience makes you a specialist or expert.

- Start to paint a mental picture of what your ideal niche or passion connection looks like, and craft an outline and script to describe them. Create a template and information profile where you develop talking points as you continue the discussion. This can include demographics, business and occupation, passion and hobbies enjoyed as a common link, and what events they might be facing in their personal and professional life. You will start to see how your talking points and discussion start to resonate with the people you meet, and you will be developing your own specific best practices.

- As you are enjoying your specific passion, hobby, or charity, start to customize your introduction statement for this particular audience when you find yourself in their company. For example, if you're a financial adviser looking to create a niche, you might say, "I help triathletes plan their retirement," or "I work with art enthusiasts to eliminate their financial anxiety so they can buy more art."

- Start attending events and speaking within the community of your interest. There's a group for everyone, as we discovered in earlier sections.

- Focus and be consistent as you add a niche component to your networking process. Another example is, "I have practiced yoga for over 10 years. I really enjoy it."

Over the years, I have met many people, strengthened my networks, and been introduced to new clients—all with a lot of time and patience.

Exercise: Where Can I Meet People?

Make a list of at least three industry-specific organizations you would like to research for joining. Use their websites to conduct your research.

1.

2.

3.

List your personal interests. How can you combine these with your professional interests?

1.

2.

3.

List at least three organizations or activities related to your interests that you would like to participate in and that you can make a contribution to.

1.

2.

3.

Make a list of five unusual places where you can talk to new people. (Have fun with this!)

1.

2.

3.

4.

5.

What is your action plan for the next three months?

Where will you go, who will you meet, and how will you follow up? (See the strategic guide in the Part 1 Appendix.)

_____

_____

_____

_____

Your own accountability questions:

Month 1

1. What did you put into action?

   _____

2. Your successes and opportunities:

   _____

3. Challenges, roadblocks, and how to improve:

   _____

Month 2

1. What did you put into action?

   _____

2. Your successes and opportunities:

   _____

3. Challenges, roadblocks, and how to improve:

   _____

Month 3

1. What did you put into action?

   _____

2. Your successes and opportunities:

   _____

3. Challenges, roadblocks, and how to improve:

   _____

Do your research. Join. Contribute. Meet new contacts!

> *"The world is a great mirror. It reflects back to you what you are. If you smile into it, it smiles back; and if you frown, it returns that greeting. The world is what you make it."*
>
> —Anonymous

3

Techniques for a Successful
Networking Event

Sarah easily registered, put on her name tag, and moved down the hallway to where she could look through the doorway and see people milling about and chatting. She suddenly got cold feet and butterflies in her stomach. This wasn't comfortable for her at all. The meeting coordinator smiled at Sarah and waved her to come inside.

"Welcome," the coordinator said. "Let me introduce you to some people."

The crowd looked harmless, and most people were smiling, but Sarah still felt uncomfortable.

You begin by taking a small step, she thought. Before she knew it, she was talking to someone and exchanging business cards. She moved through the crowd, briefly joined a small group, and then talked with three different people one on one. She even got into a conversation while moving along the refreshment table that introduced her to three more people and turned out to be one of the most productive moments of the evening.

Taking that plunge had been the hardest part, yet once she got started, she was connecting and making new contacts throughout the evening. Being prepared made all the difference.

Maybe you would feel the same at first and, in a similar situation, wonder, "How do I begin?"

Why does the thought of going to any type of business or industry event, or even a regional meeting for your firm, sometimes seem so daunting? Often it is because you feel you have to put yourself in an uncomfortable position with pressure to *network*. You might not know how to engage in this activity correctly, and you might still think of the word *networking* as being negative. I've even seen people break out in a sweat just thinking of what they have to do. Every gathering of people coming together is, in fact, the basis of a "networking event." You can develop a process of what to do before, during, and after an event to make it a great use of your time—and to walk away renewed, refreshed, and armed with opportunities to give and receive help.

My goal is to help people first discover what makes them feel uncomfortable and then plan the steps they will take to shift their mindset and see how networking in an event setting can be an excellent experience.

Few of us are ever taught the process of networking, or perhaps we didn't have a mentor to encourage us and show us the way. We internalize the concept that networking is just a way to learn and help others. Does it seem too simple? The issue is that many of us feel we need permission to walk up to someone at an event or in another department of our company, introduce ourselves, and begin a conversation. Many people have confided in me that they just don't know how to do it or what to do. Almost everyone asks, "How should I begin?" and "What if I look foolish before senior management?" and "What are they thinking of me?" These are some of the thoughts that bombard them.

How would you feel if your CEO announced at a meeting, "Let's all get to know each other better. I want everyone to network!" What goes through your mind when you attend a networking event at a convention, business meeting, or seminar? What is your attitude when you join an association, trade group, or interest group? Is the answer, "I think I'll just stand off to the side and see what happens," or "I'm going to meet new people today, and it's going to be a great experience." (Don't worry if you're not at the point of jumping in to meet new people, because I trust your attitude will change by the time you finish this book.)

To assess your networking comfort level at events, think about how you would answer these questions:

- Where would I start in a room full of strangers?

- How would I approach another person and introduce myself?

- How would I keep the conversation going?

- How would I even remember the other person's name?

- Would the person think I was rude if I handed him or her my card and asked for his or hers?

- What if I was the only new person and everyone else knew each other? Would they think I was intruding? Would they let me into their group?

- How would I break away from someone so I could keep on mingling?

- If I connected with someone, how would I follow up?

If you've ever asked yourself any of these questions, you're in good company. Many people who attend my seminars and workshops express these feelings about traditional networking events. Breaking old habits can be hard. When you're unfamiliar with the simple techniques of effective networking, you tend to stay within your comfort zone at these events—it's easier to hang out with friends or stand in the corner and wait for lunch to begin. Yet as we all truly know deep down inside, unless we're developing new contacts and deepening the relationships we have, great success in the future will evade us.

The next sections offer some helpful techniques for a successful networking event.

Give Yourself Permission

"You must give yourself *permission* to network and enjoy the process," I advise my clients. Many of us lack the self-assurance to walk into a new group. We create all types of self-talk and worry that we'll fail somehow or that people won't like us. We can forget that a business event is often where people expect to meet and connect with other people. That's why they are there, and adjusting your mindset to a positive one is the first step to success. Allow yourself to use your confidence to adopt a positive attitude. You will also have more confidence when you're prepared with effective techniques to use when you walk into that room full of people who *do* want to connect with you.

Preparation—Before the Event

Technology prepares us for everything! With LinkedIn, Google, or any search engine, your research gives you the competitive edge. Do the tasks discussed here. You'll feel better and be ready to meet, greet, and connect. In fact, preparation is the ultimate key, because it's one way to make sure that you feel better about yourself and have greater confidence. Just like anything important in life, preparation is 80% of success.

Do Your Research

Type the name of any topic, person, or organization into a search engine, and in seconds you have access to unlimited information. Look first for the most current material. I check the "press room" or "news center" to find the latest information, or look for the latest press release about the company, person, or industry I am researching. I often also set up a Google alert for my subject.

Read either print or electronic versions of industry, association, and trade magazines and newsletters. I find lots of articles and news items about promotions, job changes, and other news events that present opportunities for me to start a conversation with someone. The time you spend researching will be "net-worth it," and this is so easy to do on your phone or tablet.

See who will be speaking, and learn as much as you can about the speakers and their topics. If awards are to be presented, do some quick research on the recipients. Just by doing this simple research, you'll be able to develop some opening lines that will make approaching new people much easier and more enjoyable.

Think about the presentations you've had to make at college, at work, or for an organization. Networking at a structured event takes similar preparation. When you are well prepared and know your subject matter, you'll find yourself much more relaxed when meeting new people who could turn out to be great contacts.

Identify Whom You Want to Meet

Before any event, I strategically think of some of the people I want to meet and how to make that happen. As you know, if you go to a two-hour event with, say, 300 people, it would be physically and mentally impossible even to just say hello to each person. (And if you did do that, you would be what I call a "negative networker.") So identify a couple specific people or types of people to focus on (such as marketing personnel or human resource directors). Of course, it's great to identify people you already know that you can reconnect and catch up with, and possibly connect with people they know. The great realization is that you can begin to network the moment you walk in the door by connecting with the person at the registration desk who helped plan the event.

When I'm attending a meeting with a group for the first time, I often email or call the person who is organizing the event in advance to introduce myself and say that I look forward to the event and meeting him or her. I also often send a note after our conversation or exchange: I thank him or her again and ask if he or she would be comfortable introducing me to some of the members when I arrive. I did this recently, and my advance contact, who happened to be the president of the organization, was delighted that I recognized her as I walked in. She was graciously enthusiastic about introducing me to several new contacts. By the way, I knew exactly who she was because I recognized her from her picture on the group's website and also from a Google images search.

At the end of the evening, I thanked her and let her know that I'd enjoyed meeting the people in her organization. The following day, I sent her a note, and she responded with an email inviting me to the next meeting. By doing simple research in advance, which we all do, and learning something about the people I wanted to meet, I could be more self-assured and relaxed in my conversations with my new contacts. Taking the step to connect with the organizer or board member is the added bonus. Try this with your next event.

Take Your Toolkits, Intangible and Tangible

For any event, you need to be properly equipped. For networking events, I've created a couple toolkits that are easy to carry with you. They ensure that all your interactions and follow-ups will appear seamless and natural. As I say about these or any of my suggestions, remember to use what works for you and come up with a few new ideas to show your "networking personality." And if you're more of a natural networker or you feel very confident networking, these will only be a reminder for what you already carry with you.

Your Intangible Toolkit

The first toolkit, which weighs the least yet has the greatest value, includes the intangibles, or items that reflect the state of mind you bring with you to every event. Here's what to include in the intangible toolkit:

- **A positive attitude:** Come with a positive outlook. Table what happened at the office, and walk in relaxed and open to opportunity.

- **Self-confidence:** Keep in mind how much you have to offer to those you meet at this event. You're an expert in your field, and you want to share your knowledge with your new contacts. I often give myself a mini pep talk before I walk in, something like, "There's someone in this room I can help today" or "Today I will learn something new from someone."

- **An open mind:** Forget your preconceived notions—just go to give and learn, without any grand expectations. That will certainly alleviate any pressure. Think of your mind as a sponge: What great new information will you absorb?

- **Your presence:** Before you enter the event, silence your phone. Be present in the here and now, and avoid distractions. This shows respect for the people you are speaking with and for the event. When we focus on people, they focus on us.

- **Ears:** Make sure that your ears are open and you're ready to listen and learn. Talk less and listen more. We were given two ears and one mouth; remember to use them in that proportion.

- **Eyes:** Be ready to observe. Make eye contact to assure people that they have your full attention and interest. Eyes truly are the windows of the soul.

- **A smile:** This is the universal greeting and the key approachability factor. Plus, we all look more attractive when we're smiling. Research also tells us that when we smile, we become more confident and immediately approachable.

- **A firm handshake:** Show that your greeting is sincere with a firm, confident handshake. Make sure it's not a bone crusher or a jellyfish!

- **A goal for the event:** Make it specific and strategic to your business situation and needs.

- **An opening line:** Also prepare idea generators and "get to know you" questions.

- **A 30-second introduction about yourself:** Be ready to easily and confidently answer the inevitable question of "What do you do?"

Now that you have these "tools" in your kit, remember that true life networking takes place anywhere and anytime. Be prepared with your easy-to-carry intangible toolkit.

Your Tangible Toolkit

The items in your tangible toolkit prepare you to meet, connect, and follow up with ease. These are small items, but using them can dramatically improve your image with the people you meet. Your tangible toolkit should contain items such as these:

- **Breath mints:** It's only polite to be concerned about your breath. I've found that when you're talking a lot, your mouth becomes dry, and the quality of your breath deteriorates over the course of the event.

- **Hand sanitizer:** You will shake a lot of hands during any event and, unfortunately, collect a lot of germs you don't want to pass along. No need to be compulsive—just use it occasionally and subtly.

- **Business cards:** Make sure you have an adequate supply of cards in good condition and within easy reach.

- **Business card cases:** Take one for your cards and one for the cards you collect. Keep them in separate pockets. You never want to give away someone else's card accidentally as your own!

- **A nice pen:** Consider this as an accessory and part of your image. I'm always on the lookout for fun, interesting pens, since I collect them. They need not be expensive—just make sure they look good. Take two, in case someone wants to borrow yours to write a note.

- **A small notepad:** Use this to jot down what you learn about a new contact. I like to write something about each person to remember and follow up on. Don't write on the back of the person's business card, as some cultures consider this rude. Some people just type the information into their phone, but I prefer to write on a small, attractive pad. Use your discretion here. If I'm in a conversation with someone and I'm learning some new information, I often ask permission to take a few notes. No one has ever said no. Or wait until you walk away, and either write your notes for follow up or send to yourself on your phone.

- **Notecards and stamps:** I carry these so that I can write my personal follow-up notes immediately. Definitely send within 48 hours.

- **Highlighter:** I use this to highlight my name on my name tag, if possible. People always ask me, "How did you get your name highlighted so that it stands out?" It's a conversation starter.

- **Name tag:** Wear this on your right side so that people will see your name as they shake your right hand.

- **Mirror:** Take a quick look before you walk into the event, to make sure that you have a big smile and nothing between your teeth, that your hair is tidy, and that no tags are sticking out of your collar.

Have an Opening Line

Think about what you will say before you meet someone new. Prepare several opening lines, and practice them in front of the mirror at home. Then when you use them at an event, they'll easily flow off your tongue. And the more you do it, the more confident you'll become.

Here are some "opening lines" to consider:

- "I'm thinking of joining this group. Are you a member? What do you think of its programs (meetings, get-togethers, resources, and so on)?"

- "What brought you to this meeting?"

- "This is my first time at this meeting. What can you tell me about this group?"

- "How does this first meeting at this convention (seminar, conference) compare to others you've attended?"

- "How have you found these meetings to be helpful to your business?"

- "Have you heard the speaker before? What do you know about her?"

- "What are some of the benefits of this association?"

- "That's a great suit (tie, pin, bracelet, and so on). Where did you get it?" or "What is the story behind it?"

- "Hello, I don't think we've met yet. I'm (name), and you are...?"

Notice that most of these are open-ended questions, which require more than a one-word answer. The tip is to start the other person talking and to begin a conversation. When you've done your homework, you might even know something about the person you are meeting and be able to ask a pertinent question about his or her work or interests. This breaks the ice, and the conversation starts to flow.

My friend Barbara uses this unusual yet effective icebreaker to kill two birds with one stone. When she meets someone and learns the person's name (Tom, in this case), she immediately says, "So nice to meet you, Tom." Then she uses his name again a few minutes later, as she talks about how hard it can be to remember names and how she has been working on this for some time. She reveals that one of the things she has learned is to repeat the name. She and Tom get into a conversation about remembering names, and guess what? Not only has she broken the ice, but she's also sure to remember Tom's name! I also ask how to spell the person's name. I have clients who spell their names differently, as in Scot, Jon, and Ric. This helps me remember their name and spell it correctly when I do follow up.

Have a List of "Get to Know You" Questions

Opening lines help you enter a conversation; "get to know you" questions are different. They focus on the person you're speaking with instead of the event or organization, and they help you develop a more personal relationship that grows your network.

Two years ago, I was in Europe to give a workshop and speech at a conference. As I entered the auditorium, there was a room full of people all staring at either their notes or at me. They were early, so as I was setting up, I said, "Take this opportunity to get to know the people around you." I was pleased, of course, to see that many people were already becoming engaged in conversation.

Yet for some, you would have thought I had asked them to give a State of the Union address! Some sat in silence. One woman finally said, "It can be uncomfortable." I said, "I understand—so what if you just turn to someone you haven't met, introduce yourself, and ask why he or she came to this session? Have some fun, and remember that this room is almost like a laboratory class."

By the way, the workshop was titled *Networking to Build New Relationships*. Knowing that people love to follow specific instructions, I asked them to turn to their neighbors and ask one or more of the following questions:

- Why did you come to this session?

- Where do you live?

- Where do you work, and what do you do?

- How can someone know when a company might need the services you or your company provides?

- What do you do when you're not working? Do you have any hobbies or special interests?

- What do you most enjoy about your work?

- What types of projects do you get involved in, and what have you done recently?

- What are some of the trends going on in your field?

At first, many people just sat there. Then about 30 seconds later, they all started talking at once and kept at it. It was hard to get them to stop so I could start the session. When I finally got their attention again, I asked one of my favorite questions: "Who just met someone interesting?" Of course, every hand went up. Then I asked them to share a few things they had learned about each other. People discovered they had friends in common, grew up in the same neighborhoods, and had shared interests and hobbies. More important to their business lives, they met colleagues who could help with projects, learned about parts of the company they had never known, and discovered how they could become a resource for others.

Develop your own set of "get to know you" questions using these as a guide. Add questions relating to family, travel, hobbies, favorite books and movies, and the like. Add business-related questions appropriate to the situation. Use them at your next event, and I guarantee you'll meet someone interesting.

Develop a List of Idea-Generator Topics (Small Talk)

Some people are great at small talk. They seem to know something about many subjects and start a conversation on any of them. You can conquer small talk, too. Write down ideas as you think of them or when you read or hear something of interest to others. Become conversant about current affairs, best-selling books, movies, business news, the stock market, and certainly the latest news and trends in your own industry. Keep a journal of such topic ideas, organized by subject, right on your phone. Develop opening lines around topics that are current and in the news.

We are bombarded by interesting news 24/7. Just be careful that a topic you start to discuss isn't too controversial—you don't really want to find yourself in disagreement with your new acquaintance. If this happens, gracefully move on to another topic that is a little less provocative.

The bonus for doing your small talk research is that you become knowledgeable and more well-rounded. People enjoy talking with people who are both interesting and knowledgeable. Small talk is also part of the exploration process in conversation that leads to discovering opportunities and common interests. As you feel more at ease with the art of small talk and learn how it helps you get to know another person, you'll see how effectively it opens the door to trust and rapport. Most of us walk with a mobile news source, so you can gather something new to talk about as you're walking in the door.

A TIP ON WHERE TO FIND IDEA GENERATORS

Read a special-interest e-zine, look at a search engine cover page for the daily news, or read one of the many blogs or tip sheets that arrive daily in your inbox.

I read the front page of the *Wall Street Journal* and Google News for a quick update of what's happening in the world. Read the industry paper or magazine related to the events you attend so that you have current information about that industry. I like to prepare by reading as many of these as I can find online.

Prepare a 30-Second Introduction About Yourself

How many times have you been asked, "What do you do?" Thousands, I'm sure. It's the most common question at a networking event and, for that matter, at many meetings and gatherings. And it's one you must be prepared to answer in a clear, concise, enthusiastic, and memorable way—all in 30 seconds or less! Think of this as your personal mini info-mercial. Remember, first impressions count, and you have limited time to make a good impression. Work at making this a brief and punchy sound bite—you don't want to see people's eyes glaze over when you're going on about yourself.

When preparing your introduction, start by answering the following questions:

- How do I want to be remembered?

- What headline and benefit statement do you want to stand out in someone's mind?

- How do you differentiate yourself?

- How can you best tell people who you are and whom you work with (your target market)? What benefit do you offer?

Create several introductions that have a core consistency yet can be customized for the group or particular meeting.

If you merely state your job title and assume that other people will light up with excitement, it won't happen. Stating only your title, position, or profession might be easy, but it's far from memorable. Don't say, "I'm an investment adviser," or "I'm vice president of sales," or "I'm a computer consultant," or "I'm a real estate agent," or "I own a consulting firm." These statements tell the other person nothing about you—and usually bring the conversation to a quick end.

When you want to make a more appealing introduction, consider these instead:

- "I help people retire early [or send their kids to college, or build their dream house]."

- "I coach salespeople on how to exceed their goals."

- "I develop winning marketing campaigns."

- "I find people their dream home."

- "I assist people in developing their financial goals."

As you build your introduction statement, try this exercise to cut the words to seven or fewer, and leave out the word *I* or the name of your firm (no one cares yet anyway). Think of this as your headline:

- Help people retire comfortably and with dignity

- Remove the anxiety from networking and public speaking

- Develop and grow small businesses

- Make training entertaining

- Help companies find executives effectively and efficiently

The key to your response to the question "What do you do?" is a memorable statement that will lead to further questions about you and your business (your 30-second infomercial). Or, in the case of my doctor, "I keep people breathing."

How to Test Your Personal Infomercial

Advertisers often test their commercials long before they go into production to see how effectively they communicate. You can do the same with your personal introduction; here's how to do just that:

- Ask yourself whether your opening statement makes the other person say, "Tell me more!" Regardless of your response to "What do you do?" or the opening of your 30-second infomercial, make your statement leave the other person wanting to know more. Sometimes I open with, "I remove stage fright," and the response is, "How do you do that?" I then respond, "Workshops, consulting, and speaking engagements." Now I can develop and build the conversation based on the interests of the other person. Often I am asked who attends or books these workshops, seminars, and speaking engagements. This gives me an opportunity to describe my target audience. Yet before I do that, I usually switch gears and ask the person about him- or herself—I find out what the person does and in what industry. Listening intently and for key-words, I can then, when given back the opportunity, describe one of my target audiences; it might be in the same industry, or the other person might know someone in that industry.

- Determine whether you are specific enough. Paint a word picture in the other person's mind. We all meet many people—take the time to differentiate yourself. You don't want to be just one in a sea of names that all end up underwater. Here are two examples—one bad and one good—of putting a picture in the mind of the other person:

    Hard to see: "I'm a nutritionist, and I create diet plans with supplements to help people lose weight."

    Easy to visualize: "I help people get and stay in control of their eating patterns. I helped one woman go from 250 pounds to 140 pounds. One man had a 42-inch waist, and now size 34 pants are loose on him."

Staying enthusiastic and upbeat is key. Do you enjoy what you do, and does it show? When you're excited about your work or professional interests, you'll naturally come across as a passionate and energetic person. I've seen it so many times. Regardless of your personality type and whether you're introverted or extroverted, you'll come across as someone worth learning more about.

POSITIONING YOURSELF

Positioning revolves around your core marketing message, which should clearly state these elements:

- Who you are

- Whom you work with

- What solutions you provide

- What benefits you offer

- What results you produce

- What is special and unique about you

What benefits and solutions to problems do you provide? Always think of how you convey what you do as a benefit to the other person or a solution to a problem. I heard one person put it very well in communicating the problems she solves: "I work with organizations that are facing the many challenges of a slow economy." Here's another one that works: "You know how many businesses struggle to find new customers? I have a service that guarantees them new business."

Reflect on what makes you and your services unique. We all should know enough about our markets to have distinguished ourselves from the competition. Part of your 30-second infomercial should convey this information. It might be a process you use in your business, or a special type of client you service, or a brand-new product you offer. Be sure to communicate your uniqueness. Look at these examples:

- **Lawyer:** "My firm works with zoning cases for churches, synagogues, and mosques. We've helped houses of worship buy property when it seemed impossible."

- **Image consultant:** "I help people make 'million-dollar' first impressions by showing how just one good hairstyle and three attractive outfits will make them more appealing to new clients."

- **CEO of a computer software company:** "When small businesses think they can't afford powerful client-management software, they call us. We help businesses, even with just a dozen employees, run like a Fortune 500 company."

- **Book publisher:** "We publish business books for the busy executive. When someone wants best practices for customer service, she can read our books in the least amount of time to get the best information."

- **Real estate agent:** "First-time home buyers are anxious about their upcoming purchase. I take all the pressure of finding properties within their budget that they can move into as soon as they want."

Video is the game of today. Visit YouTube to watch different examples of introductions. Then practice your own and continue to refine and record. Keep updating it, and over time, it will be perfect.

Remember to be brief, be brilliant, and be ready to listen to other people as they tell you what they do; you will then be able to weave in more about your work.

DEVELOP A SOUND S.T.R.A.T.E.G.Y. FOR YOUR 30-SECOND INTRODUCTION

S   Make your introduction *short and succinct.*

T   *Think* of it in advance, and practice.

R   Remember the *results* you want to achieve.

A   Be *articulate* in your message.

T   *Time* is of the essence—20 to 30 seconds is optimal.

E   Speak with *enthusiasm* and *energy.*

G   Set a *goal* to attain.

Y   Focus on the *"you,"* meaning the other person you are speaking to.

Set a Goal for Every Event or Meeting You Attend

Most managers know how to define realistic goals for their departments and plan strategies for meeting them. Before you attend any meeting, set a realistic goal for that event, even if it is to establish contact or reconnect with two people.

A former colleague, Jerry, used to stand in a corner at company meetings and other gatherings while people around him were greeting each other and getting into conversations. Although Jerry was a highly respected executive, he suffered from severe shyness (familiar to many of us) that made him very uncomfortable in structured networking situations. Often he attended these meetings with his associate, Nick, who was extremely gregarious and social. Jerry knew he had to make business

---

contacts, and he also desperately wanted to have more interactions. Attending these events with Nick put added pressure on Jerry because he thought he couldn't keep up with him.

"Begin slowly," I told him. "Set a goal before you leave the office to meet at least two new people. Plan on meeting just two new people with whom you will engage in conversation, ask some open-ended questions, and exchange pleasantries." I told Jerry that he could meet more people, if he wanted, but his goal was at least two. And if he felt there was a reason to meet again, I suggested that he send a note or email or place a call to set up a follow-up meeting over breakfast or lunch. In any event, he should send a short thank you to the two people for their time and conversation. (If he had his tangible networking kit handy with its note cards, he'd be set.)

The key for Jerry—and for you—is to set a goal to make a specific number of quality connections (Jerry's goal was two) at every meeting, gathering, or event you attend. Two is a realistic goal for everyone. Think quality rather than quantity.

In the discovery conversation, I told Jerry to concentrate on four things as he connected with people:

1. Learn something new—names, what they do, why they are there, and whatever they share with you.

2. Give back a comment based on something they said, perhaps a suggestion or just a thought.

3. Take something away. If the conversation is progressing, you might take away the opportunity to talk further and get permission to follow up in the other person's preferred method of communication.

4. Think of your follow-up action plan, and implement it within 24 to 48 hours. Make this a note, an email, a text, or a similar communication.

BE THE "APPROACHER" MORE OFTEN THAN AN "APPROACHEE"

Even if you're shy (and 20% of us are), take a risk and make it your goal to approach two people. In one of my workshop exercises to help people meet each other, I say, "Take two minutes and meet someone new. Ask the people who they are and where they work; if they're in your organization, ask what department they work in and ask what comes to mind when they hear the word *networking*." I then ask everyone, "Who approached whom first?" Usually the people who were approached felt happy and complimented that someone had chosen them. I then say, "Use this technique and, at every event, you'll start to enjoy this part of networking." By being the approacher, you'll be a better networker and you'll make others feel better and more comfortable. Take the initiative.

Arrival: Take a Deep Breath

You made it to the event. You did your research; you have opening lines, you've identified small talk topics, and you've polished your 30-second infomercial. You're now ready to connect.

Introduce Yourself to the Host

Usually, one of the jobs of the host is to introduce people to each other, especially when new members or visitors are thinking of joining the group. You did your research and know who to find in the crowd. So find the host or designated greeter and ask for help. A major bonus here comes from dropping this person a note in advance saying that you're attending the meeting and that you hope he or she can help you meet several people. This shows your appreciation for the person's time and your enthusiasm for the event in advance. The host or greeter just might be ready for you when you arrive.

One night at an association event cocktail party, I lingered after checking in and, after reading the name tag on a woman at the registration desk, said, "Barbara, it's nice to meet you. I've read your organization's e-zine, and it sounds like you have a lot of active members. May I ask your help in introducing me to a couple people here to break the ice?" She gladly took me around to several people I was able to talk with for the remainder of the evening, and I made some solid new connections. When I arrived at the next meeting, I was more comfortable and walked right over to reconnect with those I had met earlier. Of course, we'd followed up in between, and I also followed up with a short note to thank Barbara for introducing me.

Get in Line

A great strategy for meeting people at the beginning of any event is to walk to where people congregate—the bar, refreshment table, registration desk, or wherever there's a line. Most people aren't fond of lines, but at events where you want to meet new people, lines provide a natural opportunity to start a conversation with the person in front or behind you. I actually like lines. Here's an example of how networking while standing in a line worked for me.

It was 11:45, right before lunch, and there was a line in front of the ladies' room (where else?) at the restaurant where I was attending a meeting. I noticed the name tag on the woman in front of me and realized we were attending the same meeting.

"Have you come to these meetings before?" I asked her. I also complimented her on the interesting necklace she was wearing. As we chatted, I learned she was the vice president of marketing for a large New York media firm. By the time we reached the beginning of the line, we had exchanged contact information and I'd promised to send her some information about my workshops and consulting business the following week. Three months later, when she was planning a sales meeting, she contacted me and hired me to do a presentation at her event. In the time between, I continually stayed in touch with a card, a note, and a text, and I certainly had her and her organization on my Google alerts and in LinkedIn.

Now she has become a valued client—all because we started talking in the line for the ladies' room. Just be open and aware, and realize that an opportunity could be right in front of you. Be aware of what I call my 24/7 networking mindset.

Dive into a Group

Approaching a group of people engaged in active discussion is hard to do. Look for a group that looks friendly. They might be laughing, smiling, or enjoying each other's companionship. Wait for an opening, and say, "I don't mean to interrupt, but you seem like a friendly group. I'm new here. Would you mind if I joined you?" Or simply walk up and just say in a gentle, approachable voice, "May I join your conversation?" Who could say no to that? Often when I use this approach, people smile and say to me, "You have courage. I admire the fact that you can do this. It's nice to meet you." This is something I do a lot because I walk into many places where I'm new and have to jump in. I'm also more introverted than extroverted, so I've learned to do this over time. Actually, I recently discovered that, like many of us, I'm more of an ambivert—I have the qualities of both an introvert and an extrovert. It's a continual practice in motion.

I had just arrived in Los Angeles and was going to be speaking the next day to a group of anesthesiologists on presentation skills. That's right, I was going to be talking about presentation and speaking skills to a group that normally puts people to sleep. There was a cocktail party that evening, and as I walked into the room, everyone was engaged in conversation. I looked around and saw that most of the people were talking in pairs. I usually don't dive into conversation with two people who are talking together because they're both engaged, and it's generally rude to walk up and disrupt a conversation.

Then I spotted a group of three people smiling and chatting informally. I walked over and said, "May I join your conversation? You seem like you're enjoying yourselves." They were great, and I ended up talking with the chairman of the meeting for the next day. By the time I spoke the next day, we were pals and had made a great connection. Take a risk, and you'll meet some very interesting people along the way.

Admittedly, approaching others who are already in a group isn't easy. Even with all your preparation, it can still be uncomfortable. I often give myself a pep talk before approaching people I don't know. Think of positive and interesting things about yourself, such as these:

- "I'm glad to be here because it's going to help me grow professionally."
- "I'm an expert in my field and eager to be a resource to others."
- "I'm a great listener."
- "I'm a friendly person and eager to learn and meet new people."

It's all in your attitude. Positive self-talk really works. I remember watching the Olympics and observing top athletes giving themselves a pep talk before their performance. If it works for them, it can work for you.

However, be sure to give your pep talk silently. Once, on a plane to Chicago, I was going over my notes for a speech. Part of my preparation is, of course, always a mental pep talk. After I did my pep talk, I took off my iPhone and disconnected. As the plane descended, several people around me started to applaud. I had forgotten where I was, and everyone heard me talking to myself!

NETWORKING GOES TO THE DOGS

I practice smiling and saying hello to people who are walking their dogs. People are generally friendly—and even if they aren't, their dogs usually are. Try this exercise if you're uncomfortable about approaching new people; it's good practice. Also, as you continue to see some of the same people, it's a way of getting to know them over time and perhaps making a new contact.

Start a Conversation with Your Dinner Partner

Look to your left. Look to your right. Your dinner partners could become important members of your network. At a seated meal, use your icebreaker opening lines and your idea generators, and start the conversation rolling. As my dear friend Jon would always say, business meals are certainly not about the food; they're about connecting with and learning from others.

At many events, you'll have opportunities to speak with more than just the people beside you at a meal. Here are a few suggestions to meet others besides those seated directly next to you:

- When there's a lull in the conversation, clink on a glass and suggest that the group introduce themselves to one another.

- Get up and walk around between courses to chat with other people at the table or around the room.

- When everyone has finished eating, trade seats with the person next to you or with someone seated across from you so that you can get to know others at the table.

Of course, ask your dinner colleagues for permission to do this as a way for all of you to connect and meet several others; you don't want to insult anyone by moving around. People will probably be glad you were the one to take charge and create more interaction. You'll be the hero.

During the Event, Make a Connection and a Plan to Follow Up

When you first meet someone at an event, your goal should be to make a connection and learn something about the person that will create reasons to follow up and allow you to begin to build a relationship. I discuss communicating and connecting with others and then following up in Chapter 10, "Stay in Touch." Until then, here are a few essential tips to use during a networking event.

Listen and Learn

My goal is to first learn about the other person before I talk about myself. I want to learn something about the person so that I can be a resource to him or her. Networking is about giving first—you might get something back later over time, or you might not.

Think giving and learning first and foremost. As you are speaking and connecting with someone, pay specific attention to what the person is saying, as well as what he or she doesn't say. Watch the person's body language, and listen with both your ears and your eyes. We were given two ears and one mouth to use in proportion. (Take a look at the Appendix to take a simple listening quiz and get some everyday tips on being a better listener.)

Find Out Preferred Ways to Stay in Touch

Busy people know how they want to hear from others. When you meet someone you want to stay in contact with, be sure to ask, "What's the best way for us to keep in touch?" Everyone has a preferred method of communication. I know that we use them all and that, with different generations, the communication forms and devices continually change. With email, phone, text, social media, and more as viable venues, I always like to find out the absolute preferred way for me to reconnect with someone. Again, we use all forms—I like to ask once and then file that away in my database.

I have one client who does not like email. Of course, she knows she needs it (it's still our number one form of business communication), yet she's not prompt in returning all the correspondence she receives, if at all. On the other hand, as soon as she receives a phone call, she responds immediately. Therefore, I know exactly how to communicate with her. In my contact information template, I have a *V* for *voicemail* next to her name. You'll find a full contact information template in the Appendix that you can customize and use in any way.

Another man I know rarely returns a call. He even told me, "I don't use my phone to speak." Clearly, I know how to communicate with him. He does return his emails and text messages, so I put an *E* for *email* next to his name in my contact list, with *T* listed as secondary. You might be thinking, "This is weird." Maybe—yet we all have our preferred method of staying in touch and conducting business. With any networking contact, whether a client or a prospect who wants to connect, we need to learn to follow suit. Of course, we use all methods of communication as business professionals; I just believe we're a step ahead when we ask someone, "What is your preferred method for me to use to follow up with you?"

BEING FLEXIBLE

Donna, a financial adviser, told this story about communicating with various people in her network:

She and a colleague at her firm, Michelle, were both engaged in supplying information to a client. The client clearly preferred email for communicating and wanted information quickly—he checked his email 24/7. Michelle's colleague, Joe, thought he was being a good time manager by checking his email only three times a day and was not responding quickly enough with the information Michelle needed. This was a problem for Michelle because the client needed speedy communication. The problem was solved when Joe offered to give Michelle his assistant's name and email. Joe's assistant replied quickly to Michele's emails, and the client was happy. This time Joe found a solution, but I would advise him in the future to realize that, as a service provider, he needs to alter his preferred method when he is in this role.

We often meet people who prefer a different form of communication from the one we use. If we want to build a relationship with them, we need to learn to be flexible. I'm almost always the service provider, so I always ask what the client wants and accommodate him or her.

> I heard a great line once about being flexible: "Praised be those that are flexible—you will never be bent out of shape."

It's important to ask your contact about his or her preference and make a note of it, either mentally (I don't trust my memory), on a small notepad, or in your notes section on your phone (then enter it into your database so that you'll always remember to use it when following up and keeping in touch).

Have an Exit Strategy

When you have a room full of people to meet, or even your designated two, it's a good idea to make sure that you don't monopolize people's time. (They most likely also have goals for people they want to meet.) Even when you're engrossed in a great conversation, it's perfectly polite to leave something for next time and close your conversation with a follow-up suggestion.

The other scenario that calls for an exit strategy is when you're talking with someone and you find yourself mentally counting the minutes until you can get away. We've all been there. Whatever the situation, you need some conversation enders and ways to wrap it up with grace and style. Here are a few that work well:

- "It was great meeting you, and I hope we can continue our conversation sometime over lunch or coffee."

- "Thank you for sharing the information about your new project. It sounds exciting. Best of continued success."

- "My time has already been well spent with the pleasure of meeting you. Enjoy the rest of the program."

- "I enjoyed hearing about your company and look forward to seeing you again."

- "Let me introduce you to_____. He may be a good person to discuss some of the opportunities you're working with."

- "I'm so glad we met. Lots of good luck, and if I hear of anything that might be a fit for you, I'll definitely be in touch."

Before I start my exit, I always ask for a card or see if we can exchange contact information right into our phones. I know that I will follow up with at least a short note according to the person's preferred method of communication if I've been able to get it. I usually wait until people ask me for my card instead of just giving them one of mine. Remember, I asked for their card first because I was interested and knew I would follow up. Over time, when we continue to build rapport, they will learn all about me.

In my conversation, I always aim to do the following:

- Learn something about the contact, such as the person's area of business.

- Give something—for example, a suggestion, a piece of advice, or a business idea.

- Take something away, if only a piece of knowledge and a way to stay in touch.

- Follow up—but only if you plan to act on it. Otherwise, it could have been a brief conversation in which you met an interesting person, learned something, shared, and moved on.

When you follow up with a personal connection, you differentiate yourself and start to solidify a relationship.

Also, before I disconnect, and if this is someone I feel I would like to get to know better, I always ask, "How do I know if I'm speaking to someone you might like to meet for your business?" At least now, I can keep the conversation going for another time, and I have created more interest. Who knows who I might be able to connect that person with over time?

"SORRY, I CAN'T TALK TO YOU—I'M HERE TO NETWORK!"

I had just walked into an evening event with my friend Robert at an Ivy League college event when we ran into a woman Robert knew. She looked at us both and, without saying hello, announced, "Sorry, I can't talk to you—I'm here to network!"

How sad for her. She was clearly out for her own gain and was trying much too hard to get something, certainly without giving first—and that's not to mention the fact that she made her friend Robert feel like he wasn't that important.

Had she been a smart networker or business communicator, she would have spent a few minutes chatting and catching up before disengaging to meet new people. It was such a negative incident that it left an indelible mark on my brain. Networking is not only about making new connections, but it is also about nurturing and digging deep into your current contacts that you are continuing to build. In fact, reconnecting with some of your contacts and clients can and should be a real goal for an event. Besides, it's nice to visit with old friends, get back on their radar, and create a stronger relationship. Remember, networking is about building strong relationships, and this takes time.

You've walked through the entire networking event, from research and goal setting, to your exit strategy. Make sure you arrive ready, and when you're there, start the process and accomplish your goals. We've also touched on the importance of listening. In the following chapter, you take that skill to the next level: discovering a process that transforms ordinary conversations into extraordinary discoveries to benefit your business life.

What's the point of using techniques for networking success? Success at networking functions doesn't always come naturally for many of us; it requires some planning and preparation. Without it, your network is unlikely to grow. With it, you'll succeed far beyond your expectations, regardless of your previous perceptions and experiences of networking.

Exercise 1: Setting Goals

List five goals that will help you be more successful when attending an event with a group of people you have never met.

1.

2.

3.

4.

5.

Write down what event(s) you will attend in the next month and up to two goals you have for each event. What type of research will you do, and who will you identify to meet?

Name of event: _____

Goal(s):

_____

_____

Research:

People I have identified to meet:

_____

_____

Exercise 2: Meeting People in Line

List five places where you can meet people standing in line—or anywhere in life.

1.

2.

3.

4.

5.

Exercise 3: Use Your 30-Second Introduction in Different Situations

Throughout the year, you might experience one or more of the following situations in which you want to use your introduction sound bite. Although your core information is the same, you want to position yourself a bit differently in each situation. Take a look at these situations and tailor your infomercial to address your audience.

- Industry-structured networking event
- Firm or company party
- Business-related volunteer group
- Chamber of commerce, Rotary, or any civic organization meeting, or a meet-up
- Business seminar
- Charity event
- Neighborhood association meeting

Exercise 4: Opening Lines

Opening lines are important for connecting with people. Write an opening line for each of the following situations:

1. At a holiday party, you are meeting someone from your company whom you do not know.

   _____

   _____

   _____

   _____

   _____

   _____

2. While on a plane, you want to start a conversation with the person sitting next to you.

   _____

   _____

   _____

   _____

   _____

   _____

3. While getting coffee, you realize that a key business contact you want to know, and with whom you have never spoken, is standing right next to you.

   _____

   _____

   _____

   _____

_____

_____

_____

4. You are standing in a buffet line, and you overhear some people talking about something you're interested in. How do you politely jump in?

_____

_____

_____

_____

_____

_____

5. You meet some people on vacation while on a tour.

_____

_____

_____

_____

_____

_____

_____

Appendix

The following checklist will help you get the most out of any business event where you are expected to meet and connect with prospects and other people to add to your networking universe. Your objective is to reach out, take the initiative, and make a positive impression. Your ability to capitalize on contacts and connections will be a key part of your continued career success.

Before You Go

- ☑ **Set a goal for the event.** Make it specific and strategic to your business situation and needs. Be realistic and know that, for your goal to be a reality, you have to follow up and take the action steps after the event.

- ☑ **Do your research.** Find out all you can about the event, including any interesting facts about the location, its purpose, the organization sponsoring it, and people likely to attend. Identify your reason for attending this event and determine your networking potential. Check the website to find out who the organizer is, who is on the advisory board, and what the mission and agenda are. If you are hosting, you have the opportunity to research all those invited.

- ☑ **Identify whom you'd like to meet.** Think strategically about the people attending. Set a goal to research three to five people you'd like to meet. Also consider calling or emailing ahead to introduce yourself to those hosting or planning the event—differentiate yourself.

☑ **Prepare your "opening line."** Think in advance what you will say as you meet people for the first time. Frame some open-ended questions to start a conversation:

- "What brought you here today?"

- "Hello, I don't believe we've met yet. I'm _____, from (company name)—and you are?"

☑ **Have a list of "get to know you" questions.** Prepare some questions that help you build rapport as you're connecting and keep the conversation going. From your advance research on the group, you'll already have some material to frame your questions.

- "What brought you to the meeting?"

- "I'm thinking of joining the group. Are you a member? Tell me a bit about what you like."

- "What are some trends you're seeing in your business?"

- "How would I know if I'm speaking to someone you would like to meet or someone who could possibly become a client for you or your business?"

- "How long have you lived in the community?"

☑ **Develop a list of idea-generator topics (small talk).** Become conversant in current affairs, best-selling books, movies, business news, the stock market, and certainly the latest news and trends in the financial industry and your special niche. Keep a running journal of such topic ideas, organized by subject, so that you're always prepared. Every day, read your preferred news medium for general news, industry news, and firm news so that you have topics ready to discuss.

☑ **Prepare a 30-second infomercial about yourself.** Be ready to easily and confidently answer the inevitable question, "What do you do?" Plan positive and interesting sound bites and a provocative value proposition about you and your company that will get people interested enough in you to get to know you better. Practice your sound bite so that it flows. It should vary according to the event, audience, and person you are talking with. The core message should be consistent, yet practice how you can change accordingly. Say enough to garner interest, and then move the conversation to what the other person does. As you prepare, remember to address these questions:

- Who are you?

- Whom do you work with (target market)?

- What solutions do you provide?

- What benefit do you offer?

- What differentiates you?

☑ **Decide on your signature prop.** Make it a conversation starter.

☑ **Prepare your tangible toolkit.** Keep these items handy to help you meet and follow up with ease:

- Grooming essentials. These simple items are often overlooked.

- Business cards. Have an adequate supply, in good condition.

- Two card cases. Use one for your cards and one for those you collect (keep them in separate pockets).

- A nice pen, an accessory for your image.

- A small notepad to jot down things you learn immediately after speaking with someone you will follow up with.

- Note cards and stamps. Have the note cards already stamped so that you can easily follow up immediately with a quick thank you note to those you've connected with.

At the Event

☑ **Employ your discovery process.** Think about these goals before every encounter: Learn something new, give something (such as a piece of advice or a suggestion), take away a piece of information you can use later, and find a way to follow up with those you've made a solid connection with.

☑ **Take a deep breath.** You've arrived, you've done your homework, and you're ready!

- ☑ **Be present.** Turn off or silence all electronic devices, to avoid distractions.

- ☑ **Have a positive attitude.** Be ready to engage and enjoy the prospect of meeting new people and reconnecting with those you know.

- ☑ **Have self-confidence.** Remember what you have to offer as an expert in your field and the company that stands behind you. Have your 20- to 30-second introduction prepared for this event. Think about how you want to be remembered—what is your headline and benefit statement, and why should others care?

- ☑ **Have an open mind.** Go to give and learn, without any immediate expectations—except to learn, connect, and give away something. Think, "There's someone here today I can learn from and give something away to" (such as a piece of advice or information).

- ☑ **Smile.** Have a genuine smile ready to show your interest and approachability (a smile is also a great confidence booster).

- ☑ **Offer a firm handshake and connect.** Make a positive, human connection. Keep your ears and eyes open and ready to connect.

- ☑ **Wear a name tag.** Highlight your name—it's a conversation starter. Wear the tag on your right side, to be seen as people shake your right hand, the way our eyes naturally look.

- ☑ **Listen and learn.** Ask about the other person first. Remember that true networking is about giving, without concern that you will get something back. Make a point to actively listen, and you will learn something new and useful. Listen with your eyes and ears, don't interrupt, and jot down later what you learned. (I'm amazed at the information I pick up when I least expect it.) Be sure to ask people what they do—people love to talk about themselves and their interests, and you will be remembered as a good conversationalist because you listened.

☑ **Be ready to take the initiative.** Approach others with positive expectations and genuine interest. Besides the people you identified in advance that you hope to meet, remember to say hello to these folks also, to maximize your attendance:

- The greeter and/or organizer

- People you meet in line as you are checking in

- People in line to get a drink or food

- Someone standing alone

Remember, you only have to say hello, smile, and be pleasant. You won't have a full conversation with everyone you meet—yet you never know unless you reach out.

☑ **Dive in!** Look for a group of three or more that's smiling and engaged; say hello and engage them yourself. (If it's just two people, they're already deep in conversation.)

☑ **Sit next to someone new.** Set a goal to sit next to someone new and get to know him or her. Also plan to follow up.

☑ **Start a conversation with your dinner partner.** If there's a meal, talk to the people on either side of you—and even those across the table, when feasible. Make a point to sit with new people.

☑ **Make connections and create a plan to follow up.** Have a goal to learn something about the people you meet, and create reasons to follow up and start building a rapport—and, hopefully, a relationship.

☑ **Find preferred methods of communication.** Every busy person has a preferred method of communication. Ask, "What is your preferred method of communication for us to connect?" Email, telephone, text, or even social media? Make it easy for the person to reply to you when you reach out.

☑ **Have an exit strategy.** At events, everyone wants to talk and mingle. If you've made a concrete connection, you will have your agenda to follow up (when and how). To diplomatically disengage at the event, use these suggestions:

- "It was great to meet you, and I look forward to continuing our conversation. As we discussed, I will follow up with you [when they told you to follow up] via [their communication preference]."

- "It was great chatting with you—I look forward to seeing you at another event. Thank you, and enjoy the rest of the meeting."

- "I'm very glad we met. Continued success, and when I have an opportunity or suggestion for you, I will definitely be in touch."

After the Event: Your Follow-up Action Plan

☑ **Within 24 hours, send an email to those you connected with.** Also consider sending a simple and sincere handwritten note, stating your pleasure at meeting them, your appreciation of their time, and any information you promised to send. You will differentiate yourself.

☑ **Send materials immediately.** People who follow up promptly always stand out. Send only what you promised (less is more)—you will have time to bring more as you deepen the connection.

☑ **Call or email within two weeks of the event to suggest a meeting with contacts who said they would enjoy the next step.** Be strategic in your follow-up. If someone expressed interest in further contact after the event, be the one to follow up with something specific, suggesting an activity, time, and place.

☑ **If a contact of yours provided you with a referral, be ready to tell that person of your follow-up and the results.** Let people know what happened, keep them in the loop about next steps, and offer a sincere thank you for the connection and introduction. Referrals are the key to many new and successful opportunities. Always thank the referrer and keep him or her in the know.

Remember, the event is only the starting point. To build strong connections into your universal network, you have to take the next steps to build the relationship—and to do so consistently.

Figure A1-1 Who Is in Your Network?

Networking Goal	Who?	Action Steps	Follow-up	Results

© 2013, Nierenberg Consulting Group, LLC.

Figure A1-2 Networking Action Plan

"The Opposite of Networking is Not Working"

How do you define networking?

7 Rules of Networking

- Smile
- Look the person in the eye
- Listen—I.R.A. formula
- Be aware of body language
- Reach out—be proactive
- Come across positive
- Look for common interests

Where are your strengths and areas of improvement?

5 Types of People Who Can Help Your Network

- Satisfied client
- Friend
- Someone who is a joiner and active participant
- Supplier or vendor
- Circles of Influence

Networking Strategies

- Become aware of everything—24/7 awareness.
- Have a plan and goal.
- Do your homework consistently.
- Be proactive. Get involved.
- Go global in your thinking.
- Be clear about your expertise.

© 2013, Nierenberg Consulting Group, LLC.

Figure A1-3 Guidelines for the Event

PART 2

Grow (Building on Your Strengths)

4

Listening and Learning

"Listening is the single most important ingredient and skill to effective communication and networking. Driven by the simple reality that when you listen, you learn more about others and thus create deeper rapport and relationships. Become an active and aware listener. Listening is the trump card to meaningful networking."
—Dr. Lyman K. (Manny) Steil, Chairman and CEO, International Listening Leadership Institute

As you continually find and build the key relationships in your business and personal life, you must *grow* both your business and your relationships to keep them prospering. In this section, we address the skills and tactics to do just that.

You will start to enhance your listening skills and other key communication skills to use every day of your life so that you can become the ultimate professional. You will discover the mysteries to communicating and working with all the personality types easily and with minimal effort. You will also embark on opportunities to develop and create your own "self-brand" so that you can market yourself in a seamless way anywhere and everywhere. We look at the advantage of the quiet or introverted networking style in depth, and we finally move into the key components for effective follow-up.

This section is chock full of information and materials that you can put to use immediately.

"If I listen, I have the advantage; if I speak, others have it."
—Arabic proverb

The Golden Rule of Listening

Two men were walking down a busy New York City street one day when, above the noise of the cars, trucks, and honking horns, one said to the other, "Listen to that cricket." His companion replied, "How can you hear a cricket in the middle of all this noise?" Without saying a word, the first man took a coin from his pocket, flipped it in the air, and let it bounce on the sidewalk with its familiar metallic sound. A dozen heads turned and feverishly looked for the bouncing coin. "We hear what we listen for," the first man said.

I often use this story to illustrate the importance of good communication skills—especially listening—in making contacts and building relationships. The first step in building trust and respect with your new contacts and your current network is to listen and learn. We have the opportunity to do this daily. This requires good communication skills, effective listening, and the ability to recognize and honor different communication styles and personality types.

Communication Skills for the Effective Networker

As you continue to master the techniques for meeting people and gaining more confidence, you are ready to enhance the communication skills that will help you connect and develop a relationship with those you want in your network. It's all about building rapport and learning how to interact with ease. Many of you know these skills and already use them to the utmost. Consider this a reminder as you put them into action in all your interactions.

Start with a Smile

Everyone responds well to a smile. When you meet someone, it's the most important thing you can wear. It's also the first step in building rapport. Remember to smile when you enter a room, begin a business meeting, answer the phone, and even start typing electronically. When you smile, the other person or persons become the mirror that reflects your expression. A smile can raise your spirits and even affect the way you sound.

Research confirms that there's "magic in a smile." When you have a genuine smile on your face as you walk into a room of strangers—or anywhere, as a matter of fact—you appear more confident and approachable, and a smile becomes contagious. A smile is also good for your brain: The act of smiling releases the neuropeptides that work toward fighting off stress. (Neuropeptides are tiny molecules that allow neurons to communicate. They facilitate messages to the body when we have a whole range of emotions.) We're also perceived as being more attractive when we smile, and people treat us differently. If you don't believe me, see how many looks you receive when you walk outside with the smile you're wearing right now. Be open to the power and control you have with the universal greeting of a smile.

When you speak on the telephone, I suggest that you use mirrors with the phrase printed on the case, "Can your smile be heard?" Put the mirror on your desk so that when you're sitting there talking on the phone, you can see your facial expressions. You can use the mirror app on your iPhone to do the same when you're speaking. You might be very surprised—yes, a smile can be heard. I always remember what my dear friend Florence used to say before picking up the telephone: "Have a smile on your face, and visualize the words *opportunity* and *decorum*." It's amazing how doing this changes your inner perception.

You might be rolling your eyes thinking, "How can I keep a mirror on my desk? My colleagues will think I'm vain." Don't worry. I've seen mirrors on the desks of many very successful people who are merely checking out their presentation image when they're on the phone.

Remember that a smile can disarm another person. Your face speaks volumes and encourages people either to open up to you or to walk away. It is a powerful tool to use when meeting new people in any situation, so use it to your advantage. I make it a habit to walk into every meeting, event, or encounter with a smile on my face. I've also gotten into the habit of smiling at three new people every day. It's warm and refreshing and totally diffuses any tension. Remember to be discreet, however. I live in New York City, so I advise people not to walk down the street grinning. I'm talking about sincere, feel-good hello smiles—and nothing else.

Look the Other Person in the Eye

Have you ever been talking with a person who was looking over your shoulder instead of at you? Did you think to yourself, "He doesn't think I'm important" or "She's not even listening to me"? Making good eye contact shows respect and interest, and it's good manners.

At a casual networking event, Carol, a vice president of human resources for a large financial services company, and her assistant, Barbara, talked to an external partner. During the entire conversation, Bill, the external, never looked at Barbara. He focused totally on her supervisor, Carol, whom he thought was the sole decision maker. As it turned out, Barbara actually made the purchasing decisions for Bill's services. He paid no attention to her and, when it came time to order, she gave her business to another supplier with comparable services.

Eye contact is one of the strongest communication skills we can develop. It's been said, and I believe it's true, that the eyes are the windows to the soul.

Another time I was at an event where a man started talking with me because I had just been on a panel. During our conversation, he kept looking past my left shoulder. At first I thought I had something hanging from it or a stain. Then in midsentence, he left me standing and seemed to fly over to talk with someone else. I thought it was rude, yet these things happen. It was ironic that, as I was walking to get a cup of tea, I heard my name called out, and a friend motioned me for me to join him. As I walked over, I saw my former acquaintance (the one who had left me to talk with someone he thought he could sell something to). Little did he know that the "someone" happened to be my friend. I can still see him squirming when my friend said, "Have you two met?" I smiled, and somehow Mr. Rude decided to take a more proper exit strategy with no immediate sales.

MAKING EYE CONTACT

Fifty-five percent of communication is visual. When you neglect to make eye contact, you might be communicating that you're uninterested, bored, or, worse yet, sneaky and untrustworthy. In reality, you might be shy or nervous about attending the event. If you find eye contact challenging, practice making eye contact with yourself in the mirror while you're on the phone. When you're in front of someone and can't look into his or her eyes, try to focus somewhere around the eyes between the nose and forehead. I call this area the "third eye." Soon it will become easier for you.

Remember Names

Dale Carnegie, author of *How to Win Friends and Influence People,* a lifetime classic, wrote, "[A] person's name is to him or her the sweetest and most important sound in any language." It really pays to remember names because people then know you've heard what they've said. Here are four ways to sharpen your name-recall skills.

1. Form an impression of the person's appearance, and embed it into your mind. Note height, stature, color of hair and eyes, facial expression, and any distinguishing physical features. I always remember my late friend Fred White, who had the whitest hair you ever saw. His name was easy to remember! Don't concentrate so much on dress or even hairstyle, though—these might be different the next time you meet. (I'm a perfect example of that!) Concentrate on remembering the person's face.

2. Repeat the person's name after you meet and a couple times during the conversation. When you repeat the name, two things happen: First, you make your contact feel good. Second, the name goes into your memory bank. Often when I teach, I meet many people with very unusual and wonderful names. I always ask them to repeat their names so I can pronounce them correctly.

Then I use the name several times. However, be sure not to turn it into a distraction and use the name too often in a short conversation. The best policy is to repeat it at the beginning when the person first says it, in the middle, and again at the end when you are exiting. I also ask people how to spell their name. John can be Jon, Rick can be Ric, and one of my clients is Scot. It's great to remember this, and people appreciate it.

3. Make up a visual story about the person's name. Associate the person's name with something that will remind you of it. Use your imagination and paint a story in your mind. Put the person into your visual story. The sillier the story, the easier it will be to remember. For example, I met someone in one of my workshops named George Whitehouse. I remembered his name by picturing him standing in front of the presidential White House, and he was shaking hands with none other than our first president, George Washington. Hence my new contact, George Whitehouse (an attorney, at that!). At your next meeting, take time to practice this with several new people you meet. It might seem challenging at first, yet it becomes fun and is truly a great way to remember people's names.

4. Write down the names of people as they walk into a meeting, and write a word or two describing them to jog your memory. I always do this when I'm speaking or training and want to remember the names of people in my audience so that I can address them personally. With effort and practice, you can remember anyone's name.

You Are a Star (Whatever Your Name Is...)

Once I was working for a company and had the opportunity to speak with the president of that company at a luncheon meeting. He was in the business of personalized stationery and prided himself on remembering names. You can imagine my surprise when I received a beautiful card from him a few weeks later. On the front it said, "You are a Star." The inside note started with, "Dear Angela" (oops).

NOTE TO BRAIN

Delete this phrase: "I'm not good at remembering names."

Replace it with: "I'm getting better at remembering names all the time."

Whatever you tell your brain is a self-fulfilling prophecy.

Introduce and Reintroduce Yourself

"Oh, my gosh! I hope he doesn't see me!" It's that awful feeling that comes over you when you see someone whose name you should remember, but your brain has just turned off. There's no need to panic. Chances are, if you draw a blank on the name of someone you've met before, that person might not remember your name, either. Simply put out your hand as I do and say, "Hi, I'm Andrea Nierenberg. We met at the last meeting." Most people reciprocate happily and reintroduce themselves. If not, just ask, "Please tell me your name again" or "Refresh my memory. What is your name again?" or "Forgive me, please tell me your name again." No one will ever say: "Guess!" I then repeat the name aloud, then repeat it silently several times again, and make a mental note to remember it. I write it down, too.

It's also a good practice to reintroduce yourself to those you have just met. Although you might remember their names and use them, they might have forgotten yours and will appreciate your gesture.

Be Aware of Your Body Language

A friend of mine always scratches her head when faced with something unpleasant. We might not realize we have these habits, so it pays to become aware of them. They could convey a less than positive body image. Avoid nervous habits such as blinking your eyes, licking your lips, fidgeting, twirling a strand of hair, stroking your mustache, or drumming your fingers. Remember Ralph Waldo Emerson's wise words: "What you do speaks so loudly that I cannot hear what you say."

You can say a lot without opening your mouth. Research tells us that we form perceptions in three ways: Verbal makes up 7%, nonverbal is 38%, and visual is 55% of our perception of others. Notice that body language makes up the biggest percentage. Make sure your body language communicates what you truly want to say. This is why the phrase "Actions speak louder than words" is so true.

Practice good posture. Standing tall and straight reflects confidence. Be aware of your facial expression. Your expression says a lot before you even open your mouth. Remember to look relaxed and happy to meet the person. Use good eye contact, smile, and react to the conversation with appropriate nonverbal actions, such as nodding and showing encouragement and interest. You might want to ask a trusted adviser or friend whether you do anything that could take away from creating a stellar impression. My sister, Meredith, has helped me a lot here. I remember her asking me, "Do you realize that you say *really* a lot? In fact, I counted 27 times once during a conversation!" At first, I was taken aback. Then I realized, "Wow, she's right!" I've become very aware of this and other pet phrases that can take away from my presentation. Meredith is a great help, and she certainly tells it like it is!

Your handshake is also part of your body language. A soft and floppy grip can imply that you lack confidence or are unenthusiastic, whereas a vicelike grip can imply that you are overly forceful and aggressive.

Robert E. Brown and Dorothea Johnson offer this sage advice in their book, *The Power of Handshaking*: "Handshakes reveal inner traits, personality, and motivations. The hands can't conceal messages as the spoken word can. Your hands are messengers of your subconscious mind, and whether you like it or not, your handshake will often betray your emotional state."[1]

They are very right. You want to appear self-confident, friendly, and open to your new contact. Here are some tips for a proper handshake:

- Grip the other person's hand firmly at the point where the webs of your thumbs meet.

- Shake from the elbow, not the shoulder, and just a couple times.

---

[1] Robert E. Brown and Dorothea Johnson, *The Power of Handshaking* (Herndon, VA: Capital Books, 2004).

- Hold for only a few seconds and end cleanly.

- Use only one hand. Don't use your other hand to cover the other person's hand.

Brown and Johnson call this the all-American handshake: "This is the handshake delivered by corporate executives and champions of both genders. This person makes eye contact, smiles, offers a firm grip, and two or three firm strokes. The handshake delivers a feeling of relaxed self-confidence. This is a warm and genuine greeting acceptable worldwide."

Other gestures are just as important as a firm, friendly handshake and reveal your readiness to meet and connect with new people.

B	**Breathe** deeply and consistently. This steadies your nerves and gives you a pleasant facial expression that says, "I'm glad to be speaking with you."
O	**Overtures** can speak volumes. Nod to show encouragement and confirm that you're listening. Keep an open posture to show you're receptive.
D	**Demeanor** is the part of your personality demonstrated by body language. A blank stare, crossed arms, and nervous gestures all convey the opposite of what you want to communicate. Instead, be open and receptive in your presence.
Y	*You* means, "I am focused on you." Observe how others interact, and find a way to match it. For example, if you're sitting across the table from a person who's leaning in to create a closer connection, follow suit. Don't lean back; this could say to him or her, "I'm not interested." Remember that actions often speak louder than words.

Consider a few more pointers on body language, which is truly an art and science all to itself:

- Notice the signals people might be giving out when you meet them.

- Pay attention to how close someone is standing or sitting next to you. It's also important to note that personal space is culturally fluid; what's considered close in one country is too far away in another. To be safe, always observe how closely people stand in lines when you're in another country and even when attending events that include people from all parts of the world.

- Watch the head position. Keep it in a straight position looking right at the other person. Someone who tilts his or her head to the side could be confused or even challenging you.

- Eye contact speaks volumes. People who look to the sides a lot are nervous or distracted. Look directly at your colleague. Someone who looks down at the floor could be shy, timid, or possibly upset. Some cultures believe that looking someone in the eyes is a sign of disrespect, so be cognizant of the person you're speaking with, so as not to make him or her uncomfortable.

- Use mirroring. When we try to replicate the body language of the person we're talking with, it's a sign of trying to establish rapport. Use this wisely.

- Monitor gestures and arms. If you stand with closed arms, others might perceive that you're closing yourself off—or that you're cold! Some people just have a habit of standing this way, and it can indicate that they're reserved or uncomfortable. People standing with their hands on their hips often convey impatience, so this can signal that it's time for you to wrap up the interaction, especially at an event. If someone's hands are closed or clenched, it could be a sign of nervousness.

- Watch for nervous gestures when connecting. Raised eyebrows could mean disagreement; someone who's constantly pushing up glasses onto his or her nose and slightly frowning could be in disagreement.

- Clue into the feet. A fast tapping or shifting of weight shows impatience and nervousness. If people shuffle their feet, they could be bored.

To play it safe, be sure to mentally observe your own body language to see what messages you might be giving out. You can lean in to show interest to the person you're speaking with. When observing others, be subtle. If someone doesn't look you in the eye during a discussion, he or she could be shy. Never take it personally.

To continually get better at this skill and become more aware, watch television with the voice off every night for three weeks in a row. Just by guessing what's going on from body language, you will improve your ability to read it. You can also go to your cellphone and check online for a quick description about something. I use this constantly and am always learning.

Keep in mind that each person has a unique body language, called baseline behavior. It's easy to spot a confident person—these people make prolonged eye contact and have a strong posture. They might also sit or stand very erect. Their faces often have an open and direct gaze.

Be Respectful of Others' Boundaries

The invisible boundaries around us that define our personal space vary from culture to culture. Most Americans become uncomfortable when someone is closer than 18 inches. In some countries, standing as close as we do in the United States is considered too far apart. In other places, it's too close. People's boundaries are not only an issue for travelers: America is a melting pot, so we need to be aware of the diversity within our own country.

Brown and Johnson advise: "Watch how far an individual extends the arm to shake your hand. As a general rule, the straighter the arm, the more protective he or she is of personal space."[2]

Look for Common Interests

Ask open-ended questions and listen to what others say in response. Practice your list of "get to know you" questions so that they come automatically. Phrase them so they can't be answered with a single word. And be sure to have a follow-up question ready.

Some people you meet will take your questions quite literally. "Did you enjoy the speaker?" you ask, hoping to start a conversation. "Yes," is the answer you get, followed by silence. So change your question to, "How did you find the speaker's presentation?" You might still get, "Fine."

---

[2] *Ibid.*

Then you can follow with, "What did you particularly like about it?" or "What did you think of his message?"

After you establish your common interests, the conversation will begin to flow. You can learn something from the other person, possibly give a suggestion or thought, take away contact information, and find a reason to follow up and stay in touch. For example, you might be able to say, "I have an article you might enjoy based on what the presenter talked about. May I send you a copy?"

Give Genuine Compliments

When you listen to people carefully, often they mention something they're proud of. Think for a moment and find a way to acknowledge their achievement. Make a goal of finding at least one positive trait or characteristic in each person you meet that you can compliment. It might seem awkward at first, but it will soon become second nature. I guarantee you can do this when you truly listen to the other person.

For example, I think one great accessory is a good pen. In fact, I often give nice pens to my clients and friends. I was at a meeting once and saw a woman with a beautiful pen in her hand. I commented how much I liked it. This simple compliment on her taste in writing utensils started the conversation rolling. Eventually, as we got to know each other, we found we had other, very similar preferences. I practice this continually; it's both fun and empowering, and it makes the other person feel good. Again, it must be authentic—you must truly take an interest.

I think back to a woman I used to work with early in my career. She was never one to mince words, and sometimes they came sounding less than encouraging. I remember saying to her over lunch, "You've taught me a lot with your direct, no-nonsense approach to things. I know that sometimes people don't understand you; however, I do, and I thank you for who you are." She was silent for a minute and then said, "Thank you. That means a lot to me."

As a general rule, most of us don't give out compliments as often as they're deserved. We worry that we'll come across as insincere or as if we're doing it because we want something. This is why it's so important to be genuine and to give a compliment only when you mean it. Only then will it be truly meaningful to the recipient. Otherwise, the less said, the better.

Sometimes you may give someone a compliment, and the recipient doesn't know how to receive it. This is a common reaction, but it shouldn't stop you. Most everyone likes to receive a sincere compliment, even if some of us have a hard time showing our appreciation. I have also found that some people crave public praise, whereas others prefer private praise. When I ask in my workshops about people's preferences in this regard, much discussion results. When I ask for a show of hands, it seems most people don't mind public praise. However, some people just don't want to be the center of attention, even if it's really good attention; they're most comfortable in a support role. Most likely, they won't tell you that they'd rather not be praised publicly, so if you sense that this might be the case, don't be afraid to ask. Then simply tell the person at an opportune time what he or she did well or how it impressed you. Also, a thank you card can mean the world to someone who prefers private praise. Take the time to observe and find out how people like to receive compliments and honor their preferences.

Right now, think of something you admire about a coworker, colleague, client, friend, and family member. Take a few minutes to jot down your thoughts, and share them either verbally or in a note. Make a practice of doing this frequently, sincerely, and consistently. It's a wonderful exercise.

FIVE A DAY

Look for positive attributes in the people you come in contact with during the course of your day, and compliment them. Make a goal to give "five a day." Put five pennies in your left pocket in the morning. Each time you give a sincere compliment, take out a penny and put it into your right pocket. By the end of the day, you should have transferred all five pennies—and you will have made at least five people feel good!

Talk Less, Listen More

One of the greatest compliments you can give another person is to let him or her know that you are listening to everything said. As Emerson said, "It is a luxury to be understood." Find the hidden word in *listen* using all the letters. The word is *silent*. That's what our internal voice must be to get the full impact of what others are saying. Remember that when you're networking with a new contact, it's like reading the paper. Let the person tell you his or her story so you can discover the news within that he or she would like to share.

More people have literally talked themselves out of a job or a sale by speaking instead of sitting back and actively listening. It takes real concentration to listen. I read once that we hear only half of what is said to us, understand only half of that, believe only half of that, and remember only half of that.

Great salespeople have learned to listen first and then tailor their sales presentation to their potential clients' needs as presented in the first few minutes of conversation. The same holds true for meeting new people and deepening our relationships with others. People know that you're genuinely interested in them as a person if you can tailor your comments to what they've just told you about themselves. Relate your experiences to theirs. For instance, often I say, "That reminds me of...," based on what I just heard. When one participant in a workshop told me how she often got nervous before speaking in front of a group because she felt her heart beating so fast, I said, "I totally understand. That reminds me of when I was a young girl and would have to speak in front of my class for a report. I would remember my heart beating so fast, I thought everyone could hear it." I also told her what my wonderful father, Paul, would say to me, and I still hear him from heaven: "No one can hear it beating, and just be glad it is!"

Are You an Effective Listener?

I recall a friend telling me this story about a dinner party she had attended. She'd been seated next to the guest of honor, a very distinguished older gentleman. After the meal, the host relayed a compliment to her from her dinner partner: "He thought you were the most fascinating person he'd met!" She told me she'd hardly said a word all evening to this man. "He was so interesting, I just listened." Well, I know this woman very well. She's a fascinating woman, successful in her profession, and a very effective networker. She knows that if you sit back and listen, people will tell you a lot about themselves, how they like to communicate, and what's important to them. It's a great communication strategy and tool. The bonus is that you learn a lot also. I'm curious by nature, so I take in every encounter as an opportunity to learn and observe—and, of course, listen.

Good networkers, like my friend, take what they've learned to the next step, making a real connection with people they can help and who can help them. As we build on our networking and realize the skills we need to find, grow, and keep our business, one of the most critical skills we must develop is the ability to listen and find ways to make a connection.

How Do You Rate as a Good Listener?

Consciously using active listening skills is a must. Rate yourself on a scale of 1 to 5 on these essential listening skills. Give yourself a 5 if you can answer, "I always do this with ease and confidence." Rate yourself a 1 if you say, "I rarely do this and feel awkward when I do."

1. I make eye contact. I always look the other person in the eye during our conversation and focus my full attention on him or her.

2. I ask questions for clarification. If I don't understand or need further clarification, I ask the other person to explain so that I can understand better. I restate what I think I understand, and then I ask to make sure that's the intended meaning. For example, I say, "What I'm hearing you say is..." or "Am I correct in understanding what you said is...?"

3. I show concern by acknowledging feelings. I also listen with my eyes. I use positive body language by nodding and smiling when appropriate. I am empathetic.

4. I try to understand the speaker's point of view before giving mine. I recognize that the other person is far more interested in stating his or her point of view than in hearing mine. I also realize that my understanding of the other person's point of view leads to building a better relationship and a better response on my part.

5. I am poised and emotionally controlled. I hold back from jumping to conclusions or interrupting with what I want to say when the other person is speaking.

6. I react nonverbally with a smile or a nod. I know this shows my interest and allows the person to continue without interruption.

7. I pay close attention and do not let my mind wander. I am careful not to allow my mind to take a mental excursion. I concentrate on what the other party is saying instead of formulating what I'm going to say next.

8. I avoid interrupting. Someone once gave me a great sign: "The most successful people have teeth marks on their tongue." Don't interrupt—let the other person finish. (This one can be tough—count how many times you interrupt someone or, easier, how many times someone interrupts you, and think about how it makes you feel.)

9. I avoid changing the subject without warning. I make sure the conversation on one subject is closed before jumping to the next subject. Changing the subject abruptly relays that you are not listening and want to talk about only whatever is on your mind.

How did you do?

If you scored 35–45, you're an exceptional listener.

If you scored 25–34, you're a very good listener.

If you scored 20–24, you're an average listener.

If you scored 15–19, keep working; you'll improve!

Take a good look at the areas where your rating could improve. Start to work on these, while continuing to practice the skills you've already mastered consistently. Take the quiz again in two weeks. Watch how your ratings improve when you commit to improving your listening skills.

Listening Skills Pay Off

Effective listening skills are not only critical to understanding and building relationships, they also pay off in business and life. I once asked the president of a company if he ever measured how much business his firm lost because someone didn't listen. He told me that the company once lost a million-dollar sale that he thought would be a sure thing. Two salespeople were involved in a conference call with the customer to close the deal. One didn't hear an important piece of information from the customer, and although the other one heard it, he misinterpreted its significance. The result was a lost sale.

The incidents and situations differ, yet the impact is the same: In most cases, when someone fails to listen and learn, the costs associated—in time, relationships, productivity, and money—are extraordinary.

ARE YOU ALL EARS?

Rate each on a scale of 1 to 5, with 5 being the best. Add the scores; then imagine your score on a continuum. On the very left, representing the lowest number, is a brick wall; on the right, representing the highest score, is a field of corn. Are you stuck up against the brick wall, or are you "all ears" in a field of corn?

How would the following people in your life rate you as a listener?

- Your best friend

- Your boss

- Your spouse or partner

- Your client(s)

- Your employee(s)

- Your dinner partner at the last party you attended

- Someone who is challenging to listen to (this is a tough one)

Keep this LISTEN-ing reminder handy:

L **Look** at the person (body language, eye contact)—be aware.

I **Involve** yourself in the conversation. Be present and ask specific questions.

S **Steady** your nerves and emotions. Refrain from interruption.

T **Translate** the meaning of the person's remarks. Put yourself in his or her place.

E Avoid mental **excursions**. Concentrate and be silent.

N **Needs** and **nurture** are both key in all relationships.

Interact with Ease

Think of someone you know who can walk into a room full of strangers and immediately make friends. Can you recall someone who instantly made you feel at ease when you first met him or her? How about someone who makes you feel as though you're the only person in the world when speaking with you?

If you know such a person, take a moment to think about what personal traits he or she possesses. Confident, empathetic, enthusiastic and energetic, tenacious, caring, appreciative—the list can go on.

I often ask this of participants at my seminars and workshops. Based on the answers from hundreds of them through the years, here are 10 common characteristics of people who interact with others with ease and grace:

1. They are able to make others feel comfortable.

2. They appear confident and at ease.

3. They are able to laugh at themselves, not at others.

4. They show interest in others by maintaining eye contact, self-disclosing, asking questions, and actively listening.

5. They extend themselves to others, leaning into a greeting with a firm handshake and a smile.

6. They convey a sense of enthusiasm and energy.

7. They are well rounded, well informed, well intentioned, and well mannered.

8. They know vignettes or stories of actual events that are interesting, humorous, and appropriate.

9. They introduce people to each other with an infectious enthusiasm that inspires conversation.

10. They convey respect and genuinely like people.

People at my seminars and workshops who know or observe others with these characteristics and who possess some themselves tell me they are successful at their business; have a wide and effective network of friends, associates, and contacts; and tend to achieve their goals. Let's look at these characteristics in more detail.

Confident

Bill is the president of a runner's club that meets for runs on Saturday mornings. He exudes confidence. It shows in the simplest of matters, like how he's able to silence 50 eager runners to make announcements before a run, and in far more important matters, such as how he's able to muster an army of volunteers to raise thousands of dollars at a run to benefit cancer research. His confidence is a magnet. People gravitate to him and eagerly offer their time and expertise. Where did his confidence come from? You can't buy it. If a store sold it, we'd all be in line. Confidence comes with experience and grows over time. What kind of experience helps us develop it? Not sitting still or doing the same thing repeatedly and expecting different results. To build confidence, you have to step out of your comfort zone and take some risks. It helps if you start with small steps and then keep going as your confidence grows.

You have to step out of your comfort zone to meet and follow up with the people you want to connect with at every event. Take small steps, develop a plan, and think about conversation starters and your follow-up. The more you set your intentions, the easier this becomes—and you will soon be more confident.

Compare this process to any new thing you have mastered—learning to play tennis, learning a new application, speaking in front of a group, and so on. You started with small steps and progressed as your competence and confidence grew. Most important, you had to step out of your comfort zone, take a risk, and do something different; as you continued to practice and got better at the skill, you gained confidence. Did you also notice that people were more interested in what you had to say than before? Expanding your contacts in your new field of expertise was suddenly easier.

REACH HIGHER

In my seminars, I ask everyone to stand and raise their hands as high as they can. Then I say, "Now, go an inch higher!" Everyone does it. The point is, we can always do better than our best. So keep reaching even higher as you develop your confidence.

To develop confidence, practice the skills you want to attain. Over time, the confidence you have developed in your abilities will show.

TO GROW YOUR CONFIDENCE, START WITH "BABY STEPS"

Taking a ride one lovely Thanksgiving holiday in Cape Cod, I never imagined I would wake up hours later in a hospital emergency room in Boston with 46 broken bones. During my recovery, I had a lot of time to reflect. This terrible automobile accident had shattered more than my bones. I thought I was a confident person, but it all seemed to disappear as I embarked on my journey to recovery.

For starters, I had to learn to walk again. I literally started with "baby steps." With each small step I took, my confidence grew. One day in the hospital, I was able to walk across the room using only a walker to push me along. Granted, it took 45 minutes, but it was a major accomplishment for me. The doctors and nurses were so proud of me, and I had gained back a bit of my lost confidence. Confidence grows in small increments: Inch by inch, it's a cinch; yard by yard, it can be hard!

Empathetic

An empathetic person puts him- or herself in someone else's shoes. Being empathetic doesn't necessarily mean you share another person's point of view; it does mean you are concerned about others and interested in their point of view.

Empathetic people pay attention to the details. They take the time to look at and listen to others. They observe and interpret body language. They listen as carefully to what people leave unsaid as to what they say. They have the ability to read between the lines. They can tell when a friend is preoccupied, and they respect these boundaries. They have the ability to make the other person truly feel heard and valued.

One afternoon, as I was working on a speech, I received a call from a business colleague, Susan. Although she tried to sound upbeat, I could tell something wasn't quite right. Her voice sounded vague and disconnected. I respected her nonverbal but obvious wish not to discuss what was bothering her over the phone, so I suggested we meet for coffee the next morning. It turned out she had just lost her job and was in a state of shock. Her dismissal had clearly come out of left field. Only the week before, her work had been highly commended.

I listened, observed her body language, made a few comments, and encouraged her as she began to develop a plan. Even though I didn't directly offer advice, she told me later that I had helped her a great deal. A week later, I received a call from a contact at a company who was looking for someone with Susan's skills. I made some calls, meetings were set up, and soon Susan had a new job. I like to think that being empathetic to Susan helped this process. I understood how she felt and what she wanted to do. Then, because both of us are good connectors, she was able to take advantage of an opportunity when it presented itself.

Appreciative

The quality that makes people charismatic networkers is their natural instinct to give sincere appreciation. I believe you can never tell someone thank you too many times when it is done sincerely.

You can say thank you in many ways. There's the handwritten note sent via the U.S. Postal Service. There's email, which is quick, easy, and immediate. In addition, there's the face-to-face thank you, delivered sincerely with special emphasis on the communication style of the person you're appreciating. You can also show appreciation by sending a gift. I'm a big believer in giving gifts and will share some of my techniques and resources when we get further into the book. Saying "thank you" might seem like simple etiquette, yet it's amazing what it can do for your professional and personal growth as a networker.

An email message I once received confirmed the value of saying thank you. The message was from the CEO of a company for whom I'd done some programs. His message was, "I want to thank you and compliment you on the work you've been doing for us. I also would like to share some of the flattering remarks that several of our senior people have for you...." It took the CEO just 30 seconds during his busy day to write this message, but it had such an impact on me that I kept it in my inbox for a very, very long time.

We all strive to be remembered positively by others. Showing sincere appreciation always makes a lasting impression. People want to do business with people they enjoy being with, and they seek out these people. In addition, an affirming communication has a way of leading to other opportunities.

Here's how a personal expression of gratitude led to a referral and a new client. After I thanked one of my suppliers for helping me meet a nearly impossible deadline, he said he wanted to do something for me in return. He told me about another client of his whom he thought might use my services and gave me the referral. I followed up and now have a new client—all for a simple thank you.

Tenacious

About 10% of my business has come from people who turned me down the first time. When I realized this, it was a lesson to me in how being tenacious can pay off for networking and for business.

I remember how one current client was particularly tough to win over. For three years, I called, emailed, texted, and tried to stay on the radar screen of this client, but I got nowhere. What organizations and events,

I thought, would she be likely to attend? I belong to several business networking groups I thought could be a possibility. At least if the person I was trying to reach might not attend a meeting, perhaps I could connect with someone from her company who knew her. My break came when I was giving a presentation at a meeting of one of these groups. After my presentation, a woman from my potential client's company approached and suggested I meet with someone in her company who could use my services. She offered to set up the meeting. Guess who this someone turned out to be? None other than Ms. "Never Returns My Calls."

The story does not have a happy ending quite yet. We did meet, and at first, I could tell the woman was doing it out of courtesy for her coworker and really did not want to meet with me. However, things got better as the meeting progressed, and it ultimately went from the 20 minutes she'd allotted to an hour and a half. At the end, she said, "I like your proposal, but frankly, we're working with plenty of consultants and it takes about five years for outside consultants to land work in our firm. However, you can call me [her preferred method of communication] every quarter just to stay in touch." At first I was discouraged, but then I thought, "At least I got in the door! And now, with five years to go, I'd better hang in there [as my father would say]." I sent my thank you note, and a month later, when I heard she'd been promoted, I sent her a note of congratulations. When the first quarter was up, I called her and left her a message that said, "I'm just touching base." I continued to keep in touch for another quarter or two, when, to my surprise, she called me. She awarded me not one, but two projects with her firm. I have since done more than 30 projects with the company; it's one of my largest clients. My tenacity paid off. Instead of getting discouraged, I just put on my schedule to call her every quarter and stayed in touch. I also added her to my "stay in touch" campaign (more on this later).

There's a fine line between being tenacious and being a pest. Be careful not to cross this line. Much of it has to do with getting permission to keep in touch. She'd invited me to keep in touch, so it was appropriate to follow up with the phone calls and notes. We linked in, and over time, I learned more about her. Being tenacious in a positive way means taking advantage of opportunities, as well as looking at the setbacks that come along as opportunities in disguise—and keeping at it.

Enthusiastic and Energetic

Enthusiasm and energy are contagious. When you're enthusiastic, you bring out the enthusiasm in others. If you're full of energy, the energy in the space around you rises. If you don't believe me, watch what happens at a gathering when folks are waiting for a speaker to take the floor. If the speaker arrives with energy, watch how the expressions on the audience's faces change and the room becomes "charged." Energy and enthusiasm make communication easier. It puts people at ease. It makes people relaxed and receptive to your message.

Realize, though, that enthusiasm and energy come in many forms. You do not have to be loud and excited to be energetic or enthusiastic. Enthusiasm can be a quiet passion that shines and makes people want to be a part of it.

I.A.S.M.

Look at the last four letters in the word *enthusIASM:* I Am Self-Motivated.

You have to believe in yourself and your ideas first before others will join you.

Caring

I believe that when you truly care about others and you don't expect a payback for your efforts, you will indeed get the ultimate reward. You will make others feel good about themselves and about you.

Often the act of caring produces unexpected, positive networking results. Recently, I received one of those "voice from your past" phone calls. It was from Gloria, who had been the receptionist at a company I had called on years before. I had last seen her 14 years before. She was now the vice president of marketing for another company. She'd recently read an article of mine and decided to call me about doing a project for her new company. I was quite flattered by her call and her invitation to do a project. When I asked her what had made her call me, she said, "You always made me feel important whenever you called. Moreover, you even told Jim, our president, that I had a great voice and a smile that truly came across the phone." She was right—I remember when I told him. (Remember what we discussed about sincere compliments?) She told me how she'd always remembered my kindness, and now she wanted to return the favor. As far as I was concerned, there was no "favor to be returned," for she did have a great voice, and I still remember how nice she was to me when I was calling on her company. When I complimented her, it was sincere and without a thought of any payback. Yet here it was, 14 years later, and she still obviously treasured my remark.

Effective networkers are always networking not because they "need" to, but because they want to create lifelong connections with people. They embrace networking as a way of life. They network without the thought of getting an immediate or specific payback. Effective networkers know they're making positive connections in which all parties ultimately benefit. How very different this is from the image many hold of networkers, which is what I call the "pathological networker" who engages in "negative networking." These folks never think of picking up the phone, writing a note, sending an email or a text, offering a heartfelt recommendation on LinkedIn, or extending a helping hand until they need something. They are not networking.

IT'S NOT ABOUT A QUICK HIT

You know the pathological networker. This is the individual you see at events passing out cards in a frenzy, obviously there for no other reason than to get a job or make a quick sale. A woman once walked up to me at an event, tapped me on the shoulder, and thrust her card into my hand. "I'm a photographer," she announced, oblivious to the conversation I was having with others. "Call and email me for work." Needless to say, that brusque introduction did not inspire me to communicate with her. Sadly, her approach is all too common at many functions today.

Each communication style has its own language.

Visual	Auditory	Kinesthetic
See	Hear	Feel
Look	Listen	Touch
Picture	Sound	Feeling
Appear	Discuss	Aware

Being a good listener and an effective communicator is key to showing empathy. When you hear someone say, "This doesn't sound right to me," an empathetic response is, "What exactly are you hearing to make you say that?"

An empathetic person is an excellent listener who understands and adapts to the needs of others. Being empathetic doesn't mean changing your personality. Nor does it mean being solicitous or manipulative. It is a positive, sincere, and proactive approach to understanding another person's feelings and interests. The dictionary definition of *empathy* is "the action or understanding, being aware of...the feelings, thoughts, and experience of another...without having the feelings, thoughts, and experience fully communicated in an objective, explicit manner." Therefore, to become empathetic, you need to be aware of communication styles and personality types.

Exercise 1: How Do You Communicate?

The following list contains eight essential communication skills for effective networking and life skills. Rate yourself on a scale of 1 to 5, with 5 being the highest and 1 needing improvement. Mark the skill(s) that you didn't rate highly (1–3). What's holding you back? What can you do to improve these skills?

_____ Smiling

_____ Looking the person in the eye

_____ Listening

_____ Remembering names

_____ Being aware of body language

_____ Respecting other people's boundaries

_____ Looking for common interests

_____ Giving genuine compliments

Exercise 2: Complimenting Others

Make a list of five coworkers or people with whom you associate, and write down at least two compliments you can give each person. Pick a day when you will see them all, and use the five-a-day penny exercise in this chapter. Your goal is to transfer all five pennies.

1. Name_____

_____

_____

2. Name_____

_____

_____

3. Name_____

_____

_____

4. Name_____

_____

_____

5. Name_____

_____

_____

Exercise 3: How Well Are You Listening?

I often say that listening skills are the most effective skill in being a successful business networker. Now it's time for you to see if you can retain what other people tell you.

Talk with other people in the room, at your office, or at a meeting about any of the topics we've covered so far. After you speak with them, tell them three things that stood out from what was said. Now consider the following questions:

Were you able to remember what they said?

_____

_____

_____

What did they remember about you?

_____

_____

_____

Is that what you wanted them to remember?

_____

_____

_____

How can you improve your communication so that people remember what you want them to?

_____

_____

_____

_____

_____

_____

Exercise 4: Characteristics of Best Practices of Great Networkers

Who is good? Write down the names of at least two people you consider to be good networkers. Then write down what characteristics they have that you think help them succeed.

1. _____

_____

2. _____

_____

3. _____

_____

Exercise 5: Are You Effective?

Look at the traits of effective networkers. Rate yourself on a 1–5 scale, where 5 is the highest and 1 is the lowest. Mark which ones you need to improve on (1–3). What strategies can help you make those areas stronger?

_____ Friendly and approachable

_____ Confident

_____ Empathetic

_____ Appreciative of others' help

_____ Tenacious in overcoming obstacles

_____ Enthusiastic and energetic

_____ Caring

_____ Good listener

_____ Able to rebound quickly from rejection

_____ Nurturing in relationships

_____ Appearing poised and polished

5

What Is Your Communication Style?

Communication Styles and Personality Types

Effective networkers are aware of communication styles and personality types. They know their own style, with its strengths and weaknesses, and have learned to recognize and honor other people's styles of communication and personality types. They also adapt their style to accommodate others, when appropriate.

How Are You Wired to Communicate?

Sometimes trying to communicate with someone who communicates differently from the way we do is like two ships passing in the night. We don't understand them, and they don't understand us.

To communicate effectively, be ready to alter the way you communicate. Once I was in France and was trying to communicate with a shopkeeper. I thought that if I spoke louder and more slowly in English, she would understand me. Of course, there was no way she could. The louder and more slowly I talked, the more frustrating it was for both of us. I needed to alter my style (talking at a regular volume in English) and try something else she could understand, such as pointing and gesturing, smiling, or finding someone who could translate for us (which I eventually did).

The frustration I felt before I altered my style is exactly the same feeling we have when we don't connect with someone else. We might even be in our own country speaking the same language, yet our communication styles are so different that we have a hard time making a connection. We need to understand and adapt our style to communicate effectively.

I'm a bottom-line person. Often I see the big picture first and then find a way to go for it, sometimes without thinking it through completely.

My friend Steve, on the other hand, is a process person. He looks at every detail, weighs both the positive and negative, and really thinks it through. Another fellow who works with Steve is even more of a process person! I have learned to communicate with them so much better now. I take the time to listen and hear every word and suggestion they give me, and I learn along the way. In the past, though, I know we all got frustrated sometimes because we wanted to communicate only "our" way. However, when we adapt, we do see things from the other person's point of view, and we can work together much more clearly and effectively. At your next meeting or networking event, practice altering your style with each person you meet or connect with. In the course of a day or event, you will most likely find yourself changing your communication style with everyone you encounter.

Everyone uses a style of communication when giving and receiving information. Harry is auditory—he learns by hearing information. He rarely takes notes at a meeting and prefers a verbal briefing to a written report. He has told me that he listens to the news every morning and night instead of reading a newspaper or online material. When I speak with Harry, the auditory type, I am sure to incorporate phrases such as, "Are we in harmony?" or "How does this sound to you?" I recognize that he will remember things he hears rather than sees, so I leave him voicemail messages instead of email or text reminders.

Ann is visual—she needs to "see in it writing." She takes many notes in a meeting and treasures handouts and written reports. She loves Power-Point presentations and videos. YouTube is one of her favorite channels. When she communicates, she often draws what she's talking about on a pad. When I talk with her, I say things like, "How does this look to you?" or "Picture this...." I know I need to paint a picture for Ann.

Bill is kinesthetic—he needs to act things out, be involved, or have things demonstrated to him. He talks with his hands and explains how to do something with a demonstration. He learns things best by actually doing them. With Bill, I say, "Are you comfortable with this idea?" or "How does this feel to you?"

Think about how you like to give and get information. What is your preferred communication style? What is that of your boss, various coworkers, your subordinates, and even your spouse? Have you ever been frustrated trying to communicate something when the other person just didn't get it? Maybe your communication styles were too disparate. Think about how you can adapt your style to accommodate the other person's. Keep in mind that people won't tell you their style. You'll learn their preferred methods only by observation and careful listening. Hear the words they use, and watch their behavior. Then you can match your words to theirs to communicate with them effectively.

Recognizing Personality Types

In addition to being aware of communication styles, a good communicator adjusts to other people's orientation or personality type. Some people are more oriented, or sensitive, to the concerns and feelings of others; others are more bottom line or results oriented. Still others are interested in and concerned with details and the way things work.

Certain ways to identify personality and temperamental categories help predict how people react and relate to each other. One popular personality style indicator many companies use is the Myers-Briggs Type Indicator. I also use the DISC profile, which explores behavioral issues. It has been around for more than 40 years and is an effective tool for understanding personality traits and styles. I definitely recommend researching these and other personality indicators. However, for you to be effective, all you really need to do is listen carefully, observe behaviors, and then respect others' personality orientation. I have found that this works time and time again. Still, it takes practice.

For example, I once walked into a corporate conference room and found myself giving three different presentations at the same time! I was there to present a training proposal to three top decision makers in the company. Having met them all, and through careful observation and listening, I knew that each had a very different personality style. My main goal (besides selling my program) was to speak to their needs and convey the benefits to each one. Therefore, I needed to adjust my presentation to each one individually. As I spoke with each person, I switched the way I conveyed the information I was giving to match his or her personality.

The head of human resources and training was amiable in her approach. What I remembered most about her was her comment to me about being sure to "get everyone involved" and her obvious caring and concern for all the employees. Clearly, I had to focus my presentation to her on the personal benefits for her employees and make sure she felt that the time her employees spent in training would be worthwhile for their growth and development.

The chief financial officer, however, was interested in the return on investment he expected from my program. In addition, he wanted details and numbers. I decided to give him the same proposal that I had given to the head of human resources, but to include a specific outline for each module, with costs clearly defined. The more data I presented to him, the better!

The CEO told me he had only six minutes to hear me out. (I actually clocked how long he was in the room, and it was exactly six minutes!) All he wanted to know was, "What are my people going to learn?" and "How much will it cost?" I was prepared with the same presentation (in case he had questions), but I gave him only the executive summary: a brief, succinct paragraph followed by bullet points and the bottom line.

These were three very different people, all wanting the same thing yet needing it delivered in three very different ways. To succeed, I had to read each person carefully and provide exactly what he or she wanted to hear.

Later, after I had done several programs with this firm, each person told me separately how much he or she enjoyed our working relationship because, "We communicate in exactly the same way." I smiled to myself, knowing that my extra work and effort to understand each personality type had been well worth it!

TRAITS OF COMMON PERSONALITY TYPES

Dominant: Bottom line oriented, competitive, direct

Makes decisions quickly

Best approach to use:

Focus on the "what"

Be efficient

Expressive:	Persuasive, animated, expressive, emotional
	Enjoys helping others
	Best approach to use:
	Focus on the "who"
	Be empathetic
Amiable:	Patient, agreeable, amiable, quiet
	Is very dependable
	Best approach to use:
	Focus on the "how"
	Be supportive
Analytical:	Compliant, cautious, accurate, analytical
	Likes a lot of details
	Best approach to use:
	Focus on the "why"
	Be logical

Not a Chameleon

An effective networker is an excellent listener who understands and adapts to the needs of others. Be aware, however, that this does not mean constantly changing your personality. Nor does it mean being solicitous or manipulative. It is a positive, sincere, and proactive approach to understanding another person's feelings and interests. You want to appear empathetic, not opportunistic. The dictionary definition of *empathy* is "the action or understanding, being aware of...the feelings, thoughts, and experience of another...without having the feelings, thoughts, and experience fully communicated in an objective, explicit manner." Therefore, to become empathetic, just be aware of communication styles and personality types.

Men and Women: Do We Network Differently?

If personality types were the only thing that made us different, that would make communication challenging enough! Take all these different types and mix in the fact that men and women perceive the world much differently—now you have a real challenge! That's right—in our diverse world, we need to take a good look at how being male or female affects how we listen to, learn from, and network with one another.

Female vs. Male Bonding

First, let's look at how the sexes relate to members of the same sex. When we see what requirements men have to feel good about their communication with each other, and when we look at how women bond with each other, we can understand what we might do to communicate better with the opposite sex. These are generalities and are useful only in providing a framework of understanding. As helpful as these can be, there's no substitute for really getting to know other people and their communication preferences. The biggest difference to remember about understanding how women communicate with each other is that women often bond more easily than men do, and in a different way.

In one accounting firm I work with, the women partners often try to give business to other women. We bond. Often by the time coffee is served, we know another woman's life story...and then we turn to business. We like to help each other once we have developed some trust.

Men tend to have some brief small talk and then dive right into doing business. They tend to think, "Why spend all that time getting to know each other, unless I know this will be a good business proposition? After the deal is done, then we can get to know each other. That will help us, since we'll be working together. If all goes well on the business end of things, and there is some mutual respect, then we might recommend each other to our associates for further business opportunities." This is what I hear from my male counterparts. We all help each other, and we do it in different ways that seem natural to us.

As you interact with the opposite sex, keeping these ideas in the back of your mind will help when you deal with any "speed bumps" in your communication. When communication is hard or breaks down between men and women, more often than not, it's because we forget there are primary differences in how we relate to each other. Remember, in most cases, both parties are trying to communicate in good faith, and it helps to consider gender differences before assuming anything different.

Men Are Thinkers, Women Are Feelers—Generally

Why do there seem to be clear and fundamental differences between men and women? Why do men tend to want to talk about external issues and women want to talk about internal ones? This has much to do with how they make decisions and determine what is important.

For example, the Myers-Briggs Type Indicator, perhaps the most widely used tool for measuring individual style and preferences, distinguishes between how "thinkers" and "feelers" make decisions and communicate them to others. Thinkers believe that the best decisions are rational, logical, and dispassionate and that everything is governed by objective, consistent rules. There are absolute rights and wrongs, and the rules can't be changed to fit a situation. They think that emotions can distort and negatively affect the quality of decisions.

Feelers, on the other hand, highly value emotion when making and acting on decisions. Their frame of reference is subjective. Making a sound decision means that everyone involved should feel as good as possible. To feelers, there are no absolute rights and wrongs. The most effective way to behave is to accommodate all styles. Their approach is sensitive to emotion and unconcerned about whether everything makes perfect sense.

Not surprisingly, two-thirds of all men who take the Myers-Briggs score highly as thinkers, and two-thirds of all women score highly as feelers. Again, these are general ideas; the important point to remember is that everyone, regardless of gender, is unique. This means that we must relate to people first and foremost as individuals.

Communication Tips Between Men and Women

If we understand ourselves and the opposite sex better, and make some slight adjustments, we'll be able to bridge communication gaps.

Listening and Body Language

The first thing that's different between us is the way we listen. Men and women do listen to each other, yet they do it differently. Women generally listen actively and often nod and smile. Men rarely do this. Men think of the nodding and smiling as agreement, seeing it as a sign encouraging them to speak. One woman I know was turned down for some business because of her continual nodding—the client thought she agreed with everything and made no decision on her own! He thought she was weak; she thought she was being polite! The client exhibited common male listening traits: wandering gaze and neutral facial expression. Many women think this is rude and inattentive. As a result, women might act defensively when men don't even realize that their listening can trigger this behavior.

A tip to women when networking with men: Cut down on the nodding and smiling, and lessen the intensity of your gaze.

A tip to men: Keep steadier eye contact and assume nothing if you see a smile or nod.

Changing Topics

Men often feel that interrupting someone is the logical way of changing speakers, while women often wait for their turn out of politeness. Women need to jump in, or they might wait a long time to speak at an event or meeting.

Advice to women: Learn to jump in—this is a skill. Speak a bit louder and faster, with more enthusiasm. Give a comment about what is being said, such as, "John, you're right, that seems relevant, and here's another point to consider." Keep the rapport going without pausing, and know that you'll be interrupted.

Advice to men: Interrupt less and wait for pauses in the conversation. Ask a woman what she thinks, and then you'll get feedback.

On the Lighter Side

Men and women look at humor and joking differently. While men may think everyone will laugh, it is not always appropriate and women may sometimes hesitate. Know your audiences and err on the side of being more conservative.

Women: Know that men exchange a lot of one-liners, and learn to follow. Just know that if the ball is tossed your way, you can throw it back. Keep it positive.

Men: Know that women prefer direct communication, such as, "Good morning. How was your weekend?" instead of: "You look exhausted. Didn't you sleep last night?"

Making Small Talk

For small talk, find gender-neutral topics, such as trends in the industry and current events rather than too much family conversation. Also, women tend to talk about themselves and their feelings more than men do. Men need to realize that this is just women's way of making small talk at times.

TIPS FOR MEN AND WOMEN TO "MEET IN THE MIDDLE" WITH COMMUNICATION SKILLS

Communication Skill	How Women Can Improve	How Men Can Improve
Listening	Keep a blank face	Maintain eye contact and listen without interrupting
Speaking	Jump in, increase volume, begin on a positive note	Wait for pauses in the conversation and avoid interrupting
Small talk	Minimize talk about yourself	Talk about something other than sports and politics
Humor	Go with the flow and learn to respond to joking politely	Avoid trying to be too witty and telling jokes that not everyone will appreciate

Tying It All Together

Building the right communication skills is a key to effective networking. These can be as simple as making eye contact and remembering people's names. Understanding the variety of personality types out there, coupled with the knowledge of men's and women's basic "wiring" when it comes to communication styles, can greatly enhance your networking opportunities. It will be a more satisfying experience for you and those with whom you network. Now that you have the basics of understanding others and making contact, we look at personal marketing—how to best present yourself in the "grocery store of life."

Exercise 1: Networking with Someone Whose Natural Communication Style Differs from Yours

Look at three emails and texts this week. Assign each a *V* (for "visual word"), *A* (for "auditory"), or *K* (for "kinesthetic"), and pay attention to the responses or reactions you receive in replies. Also pay clear attention to the sensory receivers in the messages you receive, and force yourself to reply in kind. Do this three times, and then continue being aware so that you consistently put this element into your correspondence and conversation.

Exercise 2: Networking with Each Communication Style

Fill in the following according to your style, and then look at the descriptions that follow the exercise. Think of how you will network and interact with people you meet, knowing that you have to flex your style to their way of communicating.

Communication Styles

Find your natural or primary communication style here. Even though you have one dominant style, you use all styles, some more than others. On a scale of 1 to 4, with 1 being your primary style and 4 being the style you use the least, rate the following:

The Expressive Rating: _____

You are animated, energetic, and spontaneous. You easily communicate your ideas, sometimes throwing out half-formed ideas to gather more input. You enjoy involving people. You like variety and are curious and sometimes impulsive. You could overlook details. People say you are expressive, innovative, persuasive, and outgoing.

The Amiable Rating: _____

You are empathetic, sympathetic, and friendly. You have a warm tone of voice and frequently show concern for the people with whom you work. You are very steady and caring. You are good at anticipating people's needs. You are often described as being patient, controlled, concerned, and cooperative.

The Analytical Rating: _____

You live in the world of the mind and like to keep your ideas private. You are quite deliberate. When solving a problem, you like to weigh each alternative and consider all the facts. You are organized and systematic. You tend toward perfectionism. You are detail oriented, thorough, and orderly.

The Dominant Rating: _____

You are a possibilities thinker. You value action, get impatient, and are easily bored. You are results oriented. It is relatively easy for you to make decisions and take calculated risks. You do not like to spend time considering a lot of alternatives. People say you have a lot of drive, make a good leader, and are assertive and outspoken.

The Four Major Communication Styles

Expressive:

- Be social, be able, and stay on track.

- Give special attention; plan interaction that supports others' feelings and intuitions.

- Enjoy talking about themselves, work, and style of life.

- Put what you want them to remember in writing.

- Be prepared—you will be interrupted.

- Use visuals.

- Best way to deal with these types: Get excited with them, show emotion.

Amiable:

- First win them over as a friend.

- Show sincere interest in them as people—find common interests and agreement.

- Patiently draw out their expectations and work with them.

- Present your case softly and without threat.

- Let them move at their own pace.

- Assure them that all promises will be kept.

- Make sure the closing of your visit is a logical, natural conclusion of the conversation.

- Best way to deal with these types: Be supportive, show you care.

Analytical:

- Plan your work and work your plan. Use time to be accurate.

- Approach in a straightforward, direct, yet low-key way.

- Support the logical, methodical approach. Build your credibility by listing pros and cons to the subject.

- Use comparative data and expectations to be derived.

- Be sure to answer all questions, both those that are asked and those that you think they want to ask.

- Handle all objections completely.

- Appeal to their sense of logic.

- Know that they are interested in research and statistics, and need time to think and consult before making a decision.

- Best way to deal with these types: Provide a lot of data and information

Dominant:

- Be brief, get to the point quickly, and be clear and specific.

- Stick to business. Come prepared, be well organized, and have support material that you might never open.

- Start with WIIFM (what's in it for me)—for them professionally.
- Be sure of yourself; be firm.
- Present the facts logically, and plan to be concise and efficient.
- Hit quick and hard—they make decisions on impulse.
- Bottom-line the facts.
- If you disagree, take issue with the facts, never the person.
- Close by asking for action on their part.
- Be ready to deliver on short notice.
- After talking business, depart graciously.
- Best way to deal with these types: Let them be in charge.

6

Your Best Foot Forward

I recently connected two friends. Bill is in the disability insurance business, and Joel is a Certified Public Accountant. I thought there might be some synergy between the two, and I was right: They had a good first meeting—they sincerely enjoyed meeting each other, yet what business connection might be made was not apparent.

Then we all happened to be at a business cocktail party, and as we were casually talking, Bill mentioned his supervisor. Joel's eyes lit up and said, "You work with Dan? That's great to hear! He's terrific and someone I respect a lot. Can we talk again next week and set up a time when the three of us could meet? I've read what Dan has said about developments in your company, and I'd like to share some helpful ideas that fit into your plans."

Later, as Bill and I were talking, he said, "Isn't that amazing what happened as soon as I mentioned Dan?" I said, "Yes, and it's truly remarkable when people get connected and then find something in common, and the conversation seems to flow better as your interest in each other increases." In this case, it was a true win/win situation. The connection was made.

I love sharing this phrase: *The opposite of networking is not working.* When used positively and correctly, networking can be the most important business skill you can use anywhere you go. Every time you meet someone, you have an opportunity to learn from that person and to be a resource as well. Remember, you can even learn from someone you don't like or respect, in that you can learn what *not* to do or how *not* to act. Often I say that in my workshops, and everyone agrees. We see in other people what we either want to emulate or avoid. And truly and most important, networking starts with giving—being able to find a way to help the other person.

Networking is at its best when our interpersonal skills create an atmosphere of respect and trust. We all want to do business with people who make us feel comfortable, and if we like them, that is a true home run. This chapter focuses on what it takes to present yourself as someone with character and integrity. Read the news to learn about how business leaders conduct themselves. CEOs with integrity are respected (those without it go to jail). It's about putting your best foot forward and knowing how to market yourself and build your brand.

CHARACTER CHECKUP

When you want to evaluate the character of someone with whom you'd like to connect, here are some questions to consider:

- Does the person look you in the eye when speaking, or do his or her eyes roam around the room?

- When you help someone with a referral or contact, does the person acknowledge what you did?

- Does the person answer questions honestly?

- Do you get a sense that the person is sincere, or does he or she simply see you as a business target?

Nobody is perfect; however, character does matter. Make sure the people you connect with appear to have integrity. We know that if you are reading this book and are constantly improving yourself, you certainly do. We go to school throughout our life.

Marketing Yourself

Many years ago, when I was a magazine publisher, I received a call mid-morning from one of the senior vice presidents who asked if I was free for lunch with him and the president of the division. Of course, I went. However, when I look back on all the mistakes I made, I shudder. For some crazy reason that particular day, I was going to be in the office all day, so I wasn't dressed in my normal business meeting style. I know that today we live in the world of business casual, but I realized then and there that if you want to make a great impression—you're always "on" in our world today—you have to look the part that will make you feel at your best. If that weren't enough, I was also too immature at the time to use the sage advice I have since learned: "Talk less and listen more." I came across nervous and not sure of myself instead of as someone who could have been groomed for a new job opportunity. Granted, I had the business credentials and had built a great name at my magazine, yet I didn't do a good job of really marketing myself in front of my senior management team. What a lesson I learned on the spot—and never forgot.

Fast-forward many years later. I'm still in touch with that vice president, who has since retired after serving as chairman of a major corporation. It's great to remember how I have learned over the years that you *always* have to be ready to present your "self-brand."

Think of some well-known brands that you use. Why do you always go back to them? What makes them stand out in your mind? Usually the reason you remember them is twofold: marketing and consistent quality.

We are surrounded with marketing for new ideas and products. In this book, the focus is on the opportunity to market the most important product each one of us has: ourselves. Knowing how to market and sell ourselves is the way to get noticed. Being noticed in a good way depends on *how* we do it. I find that one of the best ways is to have others believe in our brand so much that they talk about us.

The way we appear, communicate, interact, and are perceived by those in our workplace and by our clients is a direct result of the tools we develop as self-marketers. The Carnegie Institute of Technology conducted research (which other studies confirmed) showing that technical skills account for 15% of financial and career success, while interpersonal skills account for 85%. I believe that much of our success comes from our efforts to build a network of people who fully appreciate our talents, recognize our potential, and support us in getting where we want to go as we help others get what they want.

Your Personal Brand

So what is your own personal brand? It's how you express who you are and what you have to offer. Think of the vision you want to create. The brand you develop for yourself is what people will think of when they hear or see you. A brand is a reputation of credentials, and personal branding is how we market ourselves to others. Our brand ultimately serves to create an image.

Your brand will create buzz, and that informs more people about you. When you've created a recognized brand for yourself, then your clients, friends, and contacts will be your biggest advocates, and they will want to refer prospects to you. You have credibility in their eyes, and that comes from trust and believability.

Think of what distinguishes you from others in the same business. Think about what you are best known for, and write it down. Why are you known for that? Back it up with some examples.

YOU ARE THE PRODUCT

Answer these questions as you "package" your brand:

- Why did you choose to go into the business you're in? Or why are you choosing the business you want to be in?

- What types of people do you most enjoy serving and working with?

- How do you uniquely help those people solve their problems?

- With whom do you compete, and what do they do well that you should work to do as well?

- What makes you different from the competition that your current clients like?

A brand is simply what people think when they hear a name or see a logo.

As you refine and redefine your brand, always keep in mind, what do people think of when they hear your name? What immediately comes to their mind in an authentic and understood way?

Keep in mind the 10 C's of a strong personal brand:

1. Correct
2. Concise
3. Clear (less is more in your sound bite)
4. Consistent
5. Compelling
6. Clever
7. Connected
8. Committed
9. Constant
10. Current

Everything you do should be reflected in your brand, including your communications, appearance, social media presence, daily interactions, and any instances when you are speaking and writing about your brand.

You also need to incorporate your Unique Promise of Value—the feelings, words, and associations that people attribute to your personal brand. Here are some factors that will enhance your self-brand:

1. Know that your reputation is valuable. We are what we continually do and how we treat others.

2. Do what you say you are going to do. Follow up and follow through.

3. Return all forms of communication that ask for a reply, and always say thank you.

4. Treat everyone with respect and courtesy. Everyone is part of the universal network.

5. Listen. I can't say it enough.

6. Keep improving and adding to what makes *you* who you are.

THE GROCERY STORE OF LIFE

If you were sitting on the shelf, like a box of cereal, why would someone decide to buy you?

- Do you grab people's attention?

- What "ingredients" do you list that are better for the consumer?

- Are you new and improved?

Frosted Flakes has been around for many years, yet today's version is healthier and has an updated image for modern consumers. (It's okay for you to be sweet—just not sugary.)

Create Alliances

When you read newspapers, you often see stories about political and social causes that include such words as *coalition, pact,* and *associations.* These are people and organizations that join together for a common good. Joining forces brings strength and many benefits. The same is true when building your network of people.

I met Audrey, who has her own consulting business, more than three years ago at an industry networking event. After the event, I followed up with a suggestion to meet for lunch, and we have kept in touch ever since. I stay on her radar through my e-zines, tweets, LinkedIn, and marketing campaigns. Over time, we decided to create an alliance and market one another's services. Recently, Audrey called to tell me that several of her clients were interested in my services. She had made calls and sent notes to people, and some opportunities were starting to develop. I am doing the same for her. I believe that the essence of personal marketing is convincing others to believe in you and to become your advocate. This is very different from self-promotion, which often comes across as aggressive and negative.

I spoke with Audrey recently to thank her for all the connections she has started to make for me. Her answer has stuck with me: "You make me look good in front of my clients." Again, that's all the more reason to develop your alliances and connections through trust and respect. Ask yourself as Audrey did about me, "Would I want that person representing me or reflecting on my hard-earned and developed contacts and universal network?"

THE PERSONAL MARKETING ALLIANCE THREE-POINT SYSTEM

Look at how world leaders build alliances between their countries. It takes planning and patience. Look at the European Union. Years ago, it was just a dream; today it's a powerful collaboration. Here's how you can do the same:

- **Be known.** Go out and speak and write. Be a presence in your community. Be sure to keep a high profile among the people you are aligned with.

- **Be liked.** Take good care of people, and they'll take care of you. Your allies will want to hear from others how much you respect people.

- **Be trusted.** Be a true professional and always stay true to your word. Your reputation will precede you, whatever anyone says about you.

Your allies want to know from others that their association with you is an asset.

Become a Resource for Others

We all have skills and knowledge that can be helpful to others. When you become a resource for others, people will recognize your expertise, refer you, and help your network to grow.

One day I received a call from Jim, who was referred to me as someone who might help him find a job. I was happy to help him, and in turn, he offered many resources that helped me. Through our several phone meetings, I met more than 10 people and received two new projects. Jim also got his dream job through one of the connections I made for him. Both of us work our networks and believe first in giving and helping others. The result was a benefit to both of us. How do you also incorporate that into your life?

Making yourself an "expert" in an area is important. People remember what you are best known for and what expertise you have. Just think of some of the various products and services you use and why. Which product comes to mind when you think of a dependable family car? Fast pizza delivery? Delicious dinner for two? Your favorite search engine? Just as is the case with these products, your goal needs to be that your contacts see you as the *only* person who can help them in certain areas.

What skills, expertise, and resources do you have that you can give to others? How can you best communicate this? Here's a way to begin.

List your skills that you think could help others, such as persuasive writing skills, excellent computer knowledge, and social marketing expertise. I think of my IT guru, John. He's a whiz on all aspects of computers and stays up-to-date on everything, which makes my life easier. He also speaks in human terms, which is important for all of us—he makes it easy for the other person to understand him.

List areas in which you are knowledgeable. This includes specific comprehension of your industry or any new developments and trends in your field. Dr. Allan, for example, is a dentist extraordinaire. He is continually reading, taking courses, and learning new advances in the protection and care of teeth; he's always full of advice and tips on how to best care for my teeth. He never stops learning, and I'm always happy to be updated, knowing that I'm working with a pro.

Think of people, places, and things you know about that would be helpful to others—office equipment, websites, restaurants, stores, workshops and seminars, books, newsletters and recent articles, trade organizations, and the like. I continually learn new information and trends from everyone and every source in my network, and I share it with the people in my alliance to show that I am a team player. Engage in all sorts of social media, tweet, and post on Facebook and LinkedIn. Share your information with others. You will also become known over time as a thought leader.

My late friend Bruce was a master at being a resource to others. He researched 20 to 30 magazines and papers every week, both on- and offline, and sent out email memos to his database according to their interests. I was on several of his lists and always found the information interesting and helpful. What was Bruce doing besides giving out great information that he'd researched? He'd stayed on many people's radar screens, and the "buzz" about him continued. He was almost like a personal Google Alert that kept on the radar of people.

Bruce's mastery of networking went even further. He routinely sent a letter to two different people to make an email introduction and let each person know something about the other and why they would want to connect. This is an excellent exercise—it is all about creating advocates and helping each other. Again, it's so easy to implement into your weekly schedule; just keep a 24/7 networking awareness with everyone you meet and connect with. Ask how you can help them and whom you can introduce them to. Never worry about it coming back—it always does.

THE NETWORK IS ALWAYS OPEN

"The network is always open," said my friend Bruce Dorskind. He passed away shortly after he sent me this note.

Every time I venture into a store, board a train or plane, or attend a meeting, I view it as a networking opportunity. I always carry cards and a plethora of vertical trade publications. I'm not hesitant to say "Good morning" in the elevator or speak with the receptionist or security guard; I always observe what's on the desks of people with whom I am visiting. I attempt to take rigorous mental notes of important subjects. In this way, I can send relevant material, which can serve as a foundation for adding someone to my network.

I recall flying first class to Los Angeles, and I was reading 20 trade publications, ranging from a banking publication, to an engineering journal, to a magazine on Hollywood celebrities. As fate would have it, the person sitting next to me was a world-famous talent agent who was curious about my eclectic reading habits. After we established a connection, he referred me to an opportunity in the United Kingdom, which resulted in a very large fee.

Networking, like breathing, must be a natural and everyday occurrence. Everything you see on the screen, every shop you visit, and every item you read presents a potential networking opportunity. Look for those opportunities—capture them and leverage them.

Help others fine-tune their 30-second infomercials. We all need a good sounding board to test how well we communicate our image. Ask the people in your alliance to tell you what they do in a clear, concise, compelling statement. Then critique their infomercials and offer suggestions to make them better. A friend once told me in astonishment about how she overheard someone say people were describing her to others as a "specialist in landscape photography." Actually, my friend had just started a studio for children's portraits, yet in conversation she had mentioned something about her landscape photos, not her new children's studio. Although she was flattered to be mentioned to other people, she realized she had not communicated her current focus on children's portraits.

As it turns out, my photographer friend was speaking with someone who not only had children of her own (a potential client), but also was on the board of directors of a riding school that taught children with handicaps. Another photographer learned this, volunteered to take publicity photos for the school, and ended up with several paying clients. I just asked a friend who is in the final round for a position at the White House to send me his 30-second introduction on his iPhone so that I can go over it with him and prepare for the different audiences he will be interviewing with. He's a geriatric physician who also heals his patients through dance. I look forward to helping him craft his sound bite to help him win this life-changing opportunity.

Supply people in your alliance with support materials. Be sure members of your alliance have easy access to all your electronic marketing communication.

Share speaking opportunities: When you're invited to speak on a panel, in a webinar, or in any online and offline opportunity, find out whether the presenting organization needs more presenters. If so, contact appropriate people in your alliance to join you. This can even work for writing articles or creating a noncommercial, information-based website where you and several of the people in your alliance make information available.

The most important attitude with those in your close circle is to be a giver and to share every resource that helps to develop the partnership and builds greater trust.

Personal Power

Communicating a sense of inner strength comes from a belief that you are determined to reach your goals. Powerful people empower others and encourage them to express themselves openly. You communicate a sense of personal power by developing these traits:

- **Authority:** Authority is inner confidence, a trust in your skills and abilities. It comes from an attitude of "I can do that." This attitude radiates outward as you politely assert your knowledge to establish who you are while, at the same time, helping others.

- **Assertiveness:** Assertive behavior is active, direct, and honest. By being firm, we view our wants, needs, and rights as equal with those of others. An assertive person wins by influencing, listening, and negotiating so that other people choose to cooperate willingly. There's a thin line between being assertive and aggressive. When it comes across as attacking and arrogant, it's aggressive. When you're firm and getting your point across, it's assertive.

- **Accessibility:** The powerful person is a master networker. Good networking increases your visibility and provides you with a valuable circle of people to whom you can give and from whom you can receive support and information. Imagine yourself as the hub of a wheel surrounded by spokes (your contacts).

- **Image:** You communicate power through your image. How do you continually project an image consistent with strong leadership? Stand tall and walk proudly, yet with humility. Always remember that you have value as a person, regardless of anything negative people might say about you. When you meet others, make direct eye contact and keep your handshake firm and friendly. Clearly state who you are and what you do.

Confidence is a key ingredient in projecting personal power. Often I ask my classes, "Who here, besides me, would like to buy some confidence?" Almost every hand goes up. Unfortunately, confidence isn't something you can buy. You have to work at it. Confidence comes from experience—making mistakes, doing something over and over again until you get it right, and being proactive.

Think how much more confident you are today in your position than you were the first week, month, or year. How much more comfortable are you speaking in public than you were when you first took the podium? Building confidence takes time and patience.

First Impressions Count: Appearance

It takes only three seconds to make an impression. While we all believe we should be judged on our character and innate worth, unless that first impression is a positive one, we often do not get the chance to reveal who we truly are. That's why it's worth the time to look our best whenever we come in contact with those we need in our network—and that's all the time, everywhere. This doesn't mean you have to wear the latest trends and fashions. My style is to dress on the conservative side, always looking professional—and when in doubt, leave it out! (for example, avoid wearing pins for religious or political organizations). If you simply follow a few commonsense guidelines for looking your best, you can turn that first impression into a gateway to making profitable connections.

A colleague, Sarah, told me an unfortunate story that might have happened to someone you know. Sarah left New York late on a Sunday afternoon to fly to Los Angeles to present a training program the next morning. She decided to fly in comfort in a warm-up suit and tennis shoes, with no carry-on except her handbag and iPad and laptop. She checked her bag at the curbside check-in.

At nine o'clock that night, when her bag didn't come off the plane in Los Angeles, panic set in. How could she show up to teach a class on communications at nine the next morning in her unprofessional attire! Luckily for her, an all-night discount store was open, and somehow she was able to piece together an outfit. It was a miracle that she was able to look presentable when she greeted her class the next morning. However, she did confide to me that her improvised wardrobe affected her confidence. It always does. Strive to be at your best daily, no matter what.

After I heard her story, I told her my two travel rules: First, always dress professionally when traveling. You never know whom you may meet and, if something happens to your luggage, you have an outfit. Second, always carry on a bag with enough essentials to make it through a day.

Exercise: Did You Make the Connection?

After you have had a conversation with someone you want to connect with, ask yourself the following:

- Were you able to remember what the person said?

- What topics did you talk about that could lead to further connections or networking opportunities?

- What do you think the person remembers about you?

- How did the person respond to your 30-second infomercial and the other information you wanted to communicate?

- Were you able to establish a reason to make a further connection? How did it go?

- Do you know how to get in touch with the person and whether he or she prefers email, text, social media, or phone (office, home, or cellphone)?

7

Networking Etiquette

ello, my name is Linda," she said, walking over and introducing herself to Sharon, whom she met in line at an event. Without knowing how the other would react to a complete stranger, both began an eclectic discussion, ranging from Linda's childhood career dreams to Sharon's current endeavor as a personal shopper for clients interested in shopping in Paris.

After about 20 minutes, someone rudely interrupted them by standing right in front of Linda and completely taking over the conversation. The man introduced himself to Sharon as the publisher of an online magazine yet failed to acknowledge Linda. Taken aback, Linda stayed there only in an attempt to join the conversation he began about the different trends in their operating system and advertising. He never even looked at her. When the time was right (Linda's goal was to maintain her composure and redirect any negative feelings away from the situation), she injected herself back into the conversation by explaining *her* position as a media buyer. To the man's total surprise, she turned out to be a buyer for one of his top accounts.

He started to realize that perhaps he was selling the wrong person and decided that Linda was now worth speaking to. She was turned off, however, and never gave him her card or expressed any interest in talking further. She did get Sharon's card, though, and the two have stayed in touch and laughed at the circumstances under which they met.

It was truly poor networking etiquette—or negative networking, as I call it. Networking is all about establishing relationships and building trust instead of trying to make a quick sale. That never works—and it's truly self-serving and not what true networking is all about.

Two on-air stations are constantly playing in our heads. Which one you tune into more often determines how successful you are at networking. Take a listen:

- **WII-FM—What's in It for Me:** Unfortunately, this one often spells trouble because it tells the other person that you are interested only in getting something—and usually *now*.

- **MMFI-AM—Make Me (the other person) Feel Important about Me:** I work at always tuning into this station. I ask myself, "What can I do to make the other person feel good and build rapport?"

A survey we conducted asked our participants what is the worst thing someone did to you when "networking" at a traditional event. Table 7-1 shows what we learned.

Table 7-1   Survey: The Worst Things People Do While Networking

Option	Response
Seemed interested only in selling me something	44%
Left as soon as they realized I wasn't someone who could help them	26%
Talked only about himself/herself	14%
Gave advice I didn't ask for	9%
Asked too many personal questions	7%

Courtesy of Nierenberg Consulting Group

As you can see from the survey, when you tune into only yourself, others want to turn you off!

Once at a seminar, a quiet man, George, raised his hand to share his worst experience. At a cocktail party, he'd been talking with a certain woman. Later in the evening, the woman came back to him and said, "Please give me back my card. I realize that you can't help me." I know your jaws might have just dropped because, although it's true, it's difficult to believe. You'd be surprised at some of the negative networking that goes on daily. I have often wanted to record some of the incidents I've seen on my iPhone, yet I think everyone reading this book has some interesting stories!

Etiquette is good manners and common courtesy. Growing up, most of us learned our manners from our parents, school, peers, and mentors. A friend told me about a young investment banker who attended a dinner with his boss and a potential client at an upscale restaurant. Uncertain of the proper dining etiquette, he learned to survive by closely observing the manners of others. Although it worked in this situation, he knew that, to really survive in the corporate world, he would have to learn the rules of business etiquette.

I share here some etiquette tips and techniques to help you in many networking and business situations. Check your business etiquette skills with these common questions and answers.

1. At a business meal, when should I start the business discussion?

   Your answer:

   _____

   _____

   It's a good idea to let your guest have an appetizer and a beverage before starting to discuss business (or, at breakfast, let the other person have some coffee and a bite of a muffin). Use that time to get to know the person through casual conversation. Build the rapport.

2. After an initial meeting, what is the best way to follow up?

   Your answer:

   _____

   _____

   It's best to send a handwritten note over email, which most people use to communicate. Email is immediate, yet a handwritten note shows that you took the time. I often send a quick email first, and I always follow that with a handwritten note, which is my "trademark." You will differentiate yourself.

3. I'm expecting an important call. Do I leave my cellphone on during a networking meeting?

Your answer: ☐ Yes ☐ No

A: *No!*

Never leave the ringer on; turn it off and put the phone on vibrate only. Then when you feel it go off, you can excuse yourself at the right time and check for messages in private. This rule also applies to any other personal electronics that could start buzzing or ringing at a bad time.

4. I'm going to a networking event and have been advised to hand out at least 25 business cards. Is this a good goal?

Your answer: ☐ Yes ☐ No

A: *No!*

A better goal is to make a certain number of quality contacts and to follow up after the meeting. Just handing out your card is not making a quality connection. I once watched a man enter a networking event, walk around, and hand his card to the first 20 people he met. He just said, "Hi, I'm [name] with [his company name]. Here's my card. We can help you save money on [his product]." I'll bet he told everyone the next day how many "contacts" he made and how hard he "networked." I don't think so. He's an example of what not to do.

5. I'm looking for new clients. Should I send a mass email to my contact list asking for referrals?

Your answer: ☐ Yes ☐ No

A: *No!*

Thoughtfully go through your list and your LinkedIn connections, and send a personalized message or call each person you feel might be of some help or might give you advice on finding new business. Take the time to personalize this—it's a clear picture of your image and how the world receives you.

6. I would like to develop business for my firm. I know that a friend of a contact of mine knows the director of marketing. Should I use that person's name when calling for an appointment?

Your answer: ☐ Yes ☐ No ☐ Maybe

A: *Maybe!*

Do this only when you have permission from both parties, your contact and his friend. Also take the time to learn something about each of them. Be sure to send a thank you note to each and let them know what happened. This is critical and why true networking is also about the reflections back to the first source of referral. Make it positive.

Common Networking Situations and Rules of Etiquette

I was at an event and noticed Jill, an association manager, rushing into the program, which was already in progress. The registration desk had closed, so she had no name tag, was frazzled, had missed the short networking time before the seminar began, and had a hard time calming down to listen to the program. During the lunch break, she started talking to a woman in the line for drinks. When Jill wanted to give her a business card, she couldn't find them! She'd changed purses at the last minute and had forgotten to transfer her card case.

Jill was so anxious that she spent the 10-minute break searching for a stray card instead of listening to her new colleague, who eventually moved on to someone who would listen to what she was saying.

Jill hurried to another group, pushing in aggressively in her haste not to waste any more time. She blurted out her name and thrust her hand at one person in the group. Everyone politely backed away from her as they hurried to their lunch tables. During the meal, Jill just couldn't relax. She spoke too much, talked with her mouth full of food, and managed to offend everyone around her.

Poor Jill became a networking disaster at this event. What I also learned about Jill is that she doesn't do well under pressure or when everything doesn't go according to plan. What can we learn from Jill?

Following are some common networking situations and rules of etiquette that address the negative approach Jill took.

At a Networking Event or Meeting

Come prepared to your next meeting or event. Here are some reminders to make the next one seamless for you to meet, connect, and follow up.

- It's better to arrive early than late. Arriving late signals that you think your time is more valuable than the time of those at the meeting. An early arrival shows enthusiasm for the event and respect for other people's time. An added benefit is that an early arrival gives you the opportunity to meet more people. Someone once told me when you're on time, you are already late.

- Place your name tag on your right-side lapel. This places it in direct eye contact of the person you meet and allows others to see who you are and to remember your name when they are shaking your hand.

- Exchange business cards with ease. Place your cards in your right-side jacket pocket, where you can easily access them. Make sure you have enough to last through the event. Be sure they're fresh and don't look like they've been collecting lint in your pocket. Place the cards you receive from the people you meet in your left pocket. This way, you won't inadvertently give out someone else's card thinking it's your own. Or remember your toolkits and have two attractive business card cases, one for your cards and one for those you receive.

- Make eye contact—and keep it. Looking someone in the eye shows respect and interest. People can always tell when your eyes are wandering over the room looking for your next contact. Then you're are silently saying, "You are not that important to me." This isn't the message you want to communicate.

- Shake hands firmly. Nothing is worse than a fishlike or death-grip handshake. Make your handshake firm and professional.

- Be aware of personal space. Moving in too close makes people uncomfortable. Most people consider anything less than 18 inches to be too close and will back away from you.

- Join conversations in progress with grace. Be sure to ask for "permission" to join a conversation. Say something like, "This looks like a fun group—may I listen in?" People enjoy having you join them when you are courteous.

- Exit a conversation politely. Express pleasure at having met the individual and the hope that you will meet again.

- On eating and carrying on a conversation: Simple. Don't do it.

- On drinking and carrying on a conversation: A nonalcoholic drink without ice is the easiest to handle. Why no ice? Frigid handshakes aren't pleasant. Why nonalcoholic? You'll pay better attention.

Meals at Large Events or Private Functions

People were walking into the meeting room at the hotel to an industry cocktail party and dinner. Jim was very visible and audible, in that he was trying to manage his beeping digital handheld device while balancing a drink and a plate. As he walked around talking to people, he kept peering into his mobile device and kept his other cellphone in his hand, just in case it rang. By the time everyone sat down for the meal, Jim was hungry, so he started eating before it was appropriate. He tried to talk over everyone and started a conversation with one of the guests at the far end of his table, which made for an uncomfortable situation.

Unfortunately, he also picked up his neighbor's glass of water and used the wrong fork for the salad. Poor Jim—on top of all of this, he jumped right into a sales pitch at dinner, letting everyone at the table know who he was and what his company does.

Sad for Jim. (His picture should be in the dictionary next to the entry for *negative networking*.) Look over these tips to see how he might have done much better.

- Turn off your mobile device or switch to vibrate mode. Talking, texting, emailing, or, worse, making a call during a meal shows disrespect. It says, "The person I'm talking to is more important to me than you are." One woman I know thinks she is being sly by having her handheld email device in her hand and casually peering into it. Everyone knows what she's doing, and it's rude. I do also know that "everyone does it"—it's still not showing good networking etiquette.

- Introduce yourself first to the person seated to your right and your left. Then introduce yourself to the rest of the table. As others join your table, introduce yourself and others to them. You might even arrange with another colleague at the table to switch seats with you during a second course or dessert so that you both get to know more people.

- Wait for the head table to begin eating or, if it's a private meal, wait for the host or hostess to begin. When you are the host or hostess, you must begin first.

- When ordering, allow your guest(s) to order first. Direct the server first to your guest(s); then select your entrée. It's safest to pick something in the midprice range and something easy to eat. Remember, it's not about the food—it's about making connections.

- Choose your fork wisely. If you're unsure about which utensil to use, working from the outside in is the safest bet. Alternatively, watch the host, hostess, or other guests, and do as they do.

- Keep your napkin in your lap until you leave the event or restaurant. If you leave the table temporarily, leave the napkin on your chair.

- Not sure which water glass or salad plate is yours? Remember, liquids on the right, solids on the left. If your neighbor forgets and takes yours, just ignore it.

- When you're finished, place your knife and fork in a parallel position across the center of your plate. This signals the waiter to clear your setting.

- Even if you're still hungry, stop eating when everyone else is done. Slow eaters, you can always get a snack later. Conversely, if you're a fast eater, slow your pace to match that of others.

- Never talk with your mouth full. Yes, I know, you learned this when you were 6. At your next event, just watch how many adults still do this, and make sure you're not one of them.

- Refrain from talking about business until people have settled in and had their appetizers. This allows ample time for making small talk and getting acquainted.

- Ask before you take notes. It is perfectly acceptable to take notes at a business or networking meal—just ask first, out of courtesy. Then use a small, attractive notepad and pen. Always keep these in your toolkit, ready to go.

REMEMBER, YOU'RE ALWAYS "ON"

Recently, I was invited in to make a sales presentation to a company. When I met the executive vice president, I thought she looked vaguely familiar, although I couldn't place her. During my presentation, it hit me. The week before, I had been at a restaurant having dinner with a friend and had noticed her at the next table because she was yelling at the server in a disgraceful fashion. Obviously I kept this revelation to myself. However, based on the scene at the restaurant, I decided that she might be a very tough client to work with. I declined the project. The incident reminded me that we should always be on our best behavior, because, in truth, we are always "on."

We never know who's watching, and that's why 24/7 networking awareness is good to keep top of mind.

Making Introductions

At an important meeting, Bill got nervous when he ran into Mr. Davis, the president of a large manufacturing firm he wanted as his client. He was walking with an intern, Josh, who had started recently right out of college. As they approached Mr. Davis, Bill said, "Mr. Davis, I'd like you to meet Josh, who has just started with our company." Mr. Davis was professional and gracious; he spoke for a few minutes with Bill and the intern, asked a couple questions, and then made his exit. What did Bill do wrong? Here are a few clues:

1. In the business world, defer to position and age. Gender is not a factor. An introduction is normally made in a logical order:

   Introduce younger to older.

   Introduce your company peer to a peer in another company.

   Introduce a junior to a senior executive.

   Introduce a fellow executive to a client.

   Introduce a personal contact to a business contact. For example, my friend Linda accompanied me to an industry luncheon, and we found that we were seated with one of my clients. I then said to my client, "May I introduce my friend Linda? Linda, this is my client, Bob Smith."

2. When making introductions, give a brief statement about each person's interest or profession. In the best case, mention something the two might have in common. This is polite and gets the conversation going. My client Al is a master at this. As he introduces different people to me, he always tells me something about the other person and, in many cases, mentions a common interest. We then have a perfect place to start our conversation, and Al can exit gracefully.

Email Etiquette

Our work and life can get controlled by the amount of email we receive. We are constantly wired, and it's part of the new normal of today.

Although email is an essential business communication, it can be misunderstood if you don't follow certain conventions. Email lacks the vocal inflections of a phone call, the body language of a face-to-face communication, and the impact of a handwritten note on fine stationery. Yet we also know that you can tell when an email has some "attitude"—and, one hopes, a positive attitude.

Here are some email etiquette tips to make sure your recipients read and respond to your messages promptly:

1. Keep your emails brief and focused. Think of how many you get, and do the math on how long it takes to read each one. Brevity is

the winner here. Consider the fact that the Lord's Prayer is only 56 words, and the Gettysburg Address was 226.

2. Use meaningful subject lines. These are your "grabbers" and convince the recipient to open and read your message. Examples are "Thank you for your help," "Attached is an article you expressed interest in," and "Referred by...."

3. State your point as soon as possible and tell what action you want the other person to take. (Think of your email message as a mini presentation.) Be cautious, clear, and concrete.

4. When you need to send a long document, send it as an attachment.

5. Utilize the Three B's: Be brief, be brilliant, and be gone. Time is of the essence.

6. Always reread your message before you hit Send. Make sure your tone is what you want it to be. Avoid anything that could be construed as sarcasm or innuendo. Many a sad tale is told of how someone hit the button before rereading what he or she just wrote in a moment of anger, passion, or stress.

7. Answer all emails within 24 to 48 hours. A quicker response is always better. Even if you don't have an answer, at least acknowledge that you received the message and will be in touch soon. Keep people in the loop and give a status update.

8. Let people know when you'll be away. When you know you won't be able to check your email regularly, engage the automatic "away from my desk" message for your emails. Better yet, send out messages to key contacts that you will be leaving in a few days and ask if they need anything urgent before you go. As we all know, true professionals are checking even when away. Business and life go on. Stay in touch.

9. Email is never personal. Be professional at all times. Leave out emotion.

10. Have a proper introduction, body, and close with a call to action (again, mini presentation).

11. Politeness always pays—"please," "thank you," and "sorry" go a long way.

Telephone Etiquette

Although some will say that the telephone is soon joining faxes and other so-called "endangered species," we still need the phone, and it's a critical tool for interpersonal communication and human relations. In fact, I believe the popularity of the telephone and its power are coming back in vogue.

For telephone success, keep these pointers in mind:

1. Return all phone calls within 24 hours.

2. When making a call, ask if it's a good time to talk and follow the lead of the person you're calling.

3. State the purpose of your call and indicate how much time it might take to complete the conversation. If you think the call will take a half-hour, and the other person only has a few minutes, schedule another time to speak.

4. When leaving a message, state your name, purpose, and action needed clearly and succinctly. Most important, when you leave your phone number, speak s-l-o-w-l-y and repeat it. I usually write my number in the air as I say it, which makes me slow down.

5. When calling a contact referral, state your name and who referred you. For example: "Hello, Steve. My name is Andrea Nierenberg. John Baker suggested I call you about customer service training. Is this a good time to talk for a few minutes?"

6. Never do other tasks while you're on the phone. People can hear you typing on your computer or shuffling papers. This shows you're not focused on them. Even if you're just reading your email, you can't concentrate on the person on the phone. One of my clients, Roger, tells a funny story. He was on the phone one day with a client and was reading his emails at the same time. He was reading one from his wife, and when he was ready to say goodbye to his client, he said, "Bye, Honey. I love you!" Remember, doing two things at once is doing neither one well.

Avoid these voicemail mistakes:

1. Don't leave a message unless you have done your research.

2. Don't leave a long message—less is more.

3. Don't be a pest. There's a thin line between being a pest and being persistent.

4. Don't hang up without giving your connection a reason to call you back. Think about the benefit to him or her, and make your message impactful.

5. Don't speak too quickly. Don't be the Roadrunner.

6. Don't give an unrehearsed presentation. Don't mumble or be disorganized.

7. Don't be a bad listener. Pay attention to how the recipient wants information.

Non-networking Events Etiquette

Some people think that nonstop networking means making new contacts anywhere you go. Yes, you want to keep your radar up as you are meeting and connecting with people everywhere in life. Life is networking, and serendipitous opportunities pop up all the time. You have distinct advantages to forming connections at personal events, the main one being that these are people whom you've known most of your life (or their friends and relatives are), so you have a common bond. You can share a built-in sense of trust and understanding that takes much longer to develop with total strangers. However, like everything else you've learned about proper networking, there are right and wrong ways to conduct yourself.

When I want to talk business at these personal events, I keep a few ideas in mind to prevent any embarrassment:

1. Ask permission to follow up at a more appropriate time and opportunity. If I'm speaking to my friend's cousin from St. Louis and I find out she's the head of human resources training, I ask for her contact information and inquire if it's okay to get in touch at a future date and in her preferred method of communication.

2. Remember where you are. If you're at a funeral and happen to find out the person next to you is part of a chamber of commerce organization in your community, think about how to approach being invited to a meeting. Before you disengage, ask the person how best to follow up. Doing anything else would be considered very bad taste.

3. What do you do when someone else wants to talk business? If the other person is pushing to discuss business, graciously suggest, "Who would have thought we'd meet at this event? However, this is probably not the right place to discuss business, so may we connect tomorrow and see when we can discuss this further?"

4. Exchange contact information and get back to the event at hand.

5. Play by the rules. Recognize that there are establishments, such as some private clubs, where conducting business simply is not allowed. Be sure to follow the prescribed behavior.

This has changed a lot, yet always pay attention to the rules so you will be invited back.

Never Keep a Scorecard

It's always better to give than to receive, and things have a way of coming back to the giver. When you look at business leaders, from Andrew Carnegie to Bill Gates, you see how their generosity in giving to others gets them a lot of good press. The same can be true with you. When you give to others, you build up your own personal public image, which goes a long way in developing business contacts now and well into the future.

Here's my advice on keeping track of exchanging favors when it comes to networking:

1. Give more than you get. Even when someone does a favor for you first, think about how you can return it and add something extra. If someone gives you a client lead, think about how you can offer a referral and possibly a gift of some sort to say thanks for the referral and belief.

2. Continually asking for a favor in return is a big mistake. People work hard to refer people they know, like, and trust, and that takes time and relationship building.

3. Have a giving attitude. Mother Teresa is much more famous than most people in the world. She was a giver who looked at life from an eternal perspective. Be a giver, and it will come back to you in better ways than you ever imagined.

4. One of my favorite phrases is, "Give without remembering and receive without forgetting." It was one of my wonderful dad's favorite lines. He lived by it.

Social Media Netiquette

Social media networking is here to stay—and is also changing at lightning speed. The world of social media blends professional and personal communication. Keep these tips in mind to better navigate this terrain:

1. Offer something of value. Is it useful and valuable?

2. Observe people's habits before engaging with them. You may tweet a lot; another person might not. Again, find out preferred methods. The same goes with IM, LinkedIn, and Facebook.

3. Stop and think before you say something you might regret. If in doubt, leave it out.

4. Make your style clear and obvious. Many of us are glued to the Internet; others are not. Be sure to let others know your communication styles also.

5. Resist the temptation to multitask.

6. Be respectful of everyone's content and blogs.

7. Be sure your LinkedIn profile is up-to-date and 100% complete. When connecting or inviting, always add a personal message stating what you have in common and why you would like to connect. LinkedIn is your online professional resume, bio, and brand builder all wrapped into one.

8. On LinkedIn, as with Twitter and other forms of social media, think quality versus quantity.

9. Become known as a thought leader and a true professional networker on LinkedIn. Share, introduce, and stay connected.

10. Remember, all forms of social media and online networking are tools and technology that make the ultimate goal of connecting offline easier. Our primary goal of networking is to build real relationships, face to face and eyeball to eyeball. Social media helps facilitate some of our initial approaches, offers ways to stay in touch and connected, and helps us expand our networks through people we are connected with.

People build trusting relationships with others by looking them in the eye, shaking their hand, and getting that intuitive feeling about them. You can do a lot with social media, yet real chemistry is built offline. The technology is a tool to support what we primarily do in person.

THE "GOLDEN RULES" OF EFFECTIVE NETWORKING

- Respect other people's time; it's a precious commodity for everyone.

- Offer to help others sincerely. People can tell the difference between an opportunist and someone doing a good deed for people.

- Always show and convey appreciation. Gratitude can be in the form of a gift or a simple note of thanks. Either way, do it consistently.

- Share information. If you know something that can help someone, pass it on. Imagine—if previous generations hadn't shared with us their knowledge, the world could not have progressed. I learn something new daily from my universal network. It is a true gift.

- Follow up, follow through, and keep others in the loop: Avoid being a "missing in action" networker. Find a good reason to stay connected, even when there's no "breaking news." Staying in touch and connected is key.

Networking "Are We There Yet?"

Like children traveling in the backseat of a car, we often get impatient having to wait to arrive at our destination. When people network, they often think, "I made contact, I received the person's contact information, and we had lunch. So why is it taking so long to get their business?"

Generating genuine trust with someone takes time and patience. The items at the top of your priority list might not even get an honorable mention on someone else's. Many of my best networking connections that led to new business took years—yes, two to five years. There's no set time, and each situation is different.

Networking works much like bamboo grows. It takes between 4 and 15 years to grow, yet once it starts, it can shoot up to 90 feet in six weeks. What was it doing during that time? It was building a root system, much as we do as we build and expand our networks.

Remember, your personal image has to last over the long term. Think about major brands of consumer products such as Coke, Apple, and Starbucks. They took years to develop into respected names in the minds of consumers. The same is true with you. When you plant your networking "seeds" with business cards or meetings, give them time to grow. Pull an apple off the tree too soon, and it's bitter.

Put your best foot forward as you continue on your networking journey. We looked at establishing your personal brand through making alliances, becoming a resource, and showing respect for others. You know the basic rules of etiquette—although they're constantly changing, you got the basics here. In the next chapter, we tackle one of the most interesting and popular aspects of networking: how introverts can network effectively. If you or someone you know is shy when it comes to meeting new people, get ready. You'll be surprised to discover that introverts have more going for them in networking than one might think.

Exercise: Self-Evaluation for Your Best Networking Traits

Take a look in the networking mirror to see what about you shines and what you should focus on when you network more frequently. Here's one exercise to help you:

1. Make a list of three things you're comfortable doing in your business and personal life. You might say, "I'm a good listener," "I enjoy setting up meetings," or "I always send people information to help them do their jobs better."

2. Now take those behaviors and look at the strengths you bring to your work and your networking opportunities. For example, as a good listener, I'm able to hear the most important information on a call and then direct the person to other resources that can help the most. How do the things you wrote down distinguish you from others? You might find that you're more skillful than anyone else in your department in building relationships with people from other cultures.

"For lack of training, they lacked knowledge; for lack of knowledge, they lacked confidence; for lack of confidence, they lacked victory."
—Julius Caesar

8

The Introvert's Networking Advantage: The Quiet Way to Success

My friend Jorge goes to the gym early every morning and sees the same three people almost every day. He exchanges a brief hi with two of them, but never the third, and the chatting has never gone beyond the weather. He doesn't know the names of any of them, or why they come early to the gym, whether they have jobs they go to later, or anything about them.

He figures that they, like himself, would feel crowded or intruded upon if the conversation got more than superficially casual. And the woman might even think he was hitting on her. So he keeps a space or distance between them. He says it's because he's shy, an introvert. Plus—and, mind you, this is important—he has no incentive to know them better because he can envision no future moment when knowing them better might benefit him or them.

He is probably wrong. What if he's missing a connection that could someday lead to a significant business or personal breakthrough? What if just knowing them might make his life a little richer and build his networking skills for general usage?

If you relate to Jorge and know yourself to be more introverted than extroverted, you might benefit from considering Cyndi's story, which I share next.

A Quiet Networker's Success Story

When the door opened and I walked in to start a business development meeting with several executives at a firm, Cyndi clearly struck me with her approach to communication. I had heard beforehand that she was a rising star in the corporation, yet her challenge lay in the fact that she was unable to look me—or her colleagues, for that matter—in the eye. Her shoulders were slumped, she made no small talk, and as she started to talk about some of her projects, she gave just the facts in a monotone voice. Then like a lightning rod, she spoke about her newest project, which was an initiative she was starting. It was as if a different person emerged from the Cyndi we first met. Her voice changed, she came "alive," and she spoke in such a way as to paint a real word picture of what she was looking to accomplish.

What happened that transformed her from seemingly shy and withdrawn to a passionate communicator about her work? Bottom line, Cyndi is an introvert. As I got to know her, she explained some of the challenges she faced in the business world. She felt she had to be "on" continually to sell herself, which she didn't like at all. As we began to talk and work together, she saw that she could keep her own style and personality and still "market herself"—she could communicate her ideas and strengths in a positive way. As her perceptions changed, her actions did, too, along with the way her colleagues and management perceived her.

I've known Cyndi for 10 years now, and she is currently a senior vice president of another large corporation, where she runs a whole business unit and frequently speaks around the country. When I visit with her, she always goes back to the time when we first met, when she never thought she would be able to come out of her shell.

One way that I always spot the Cyndis, Jorges, or other quiet networkers and communicators when I do a workshop is by the response I get from my first question on my prework questionnaire: "When you hear the word *networking*, what immediately comes to mind? How do you feel about networking for your career advancement?"

This icebreaker is very telling. People pour out their feelings, and what I usually hear is: "I hate it. I'm not good at it," or "I don't like having to sell myself" or "It's not me."

If you're like Cyndi, Jorge, or any of those people who feel uncomfortable extending yourself into what you view as other people's space, then the first step is to realize that networking is a state of mind. You continually network in the way you interact, connect, and build on your relationships, regardless of your style. What you might view as just the way you are or as a personal weakness might actually be a strength you can use to your advantage, to get started on the road to positive personal marketing. There's a way even you, as an introvert, can work in the most passionate and organized way, follow up with efficiency, and develop alliances with others in the organization who will market you.

The Introvert's Business Advantage

Did you know that Albert Einstein, Socrates, Mahatma Gandhi, Angelina Jolie, and Colin Powell are all introverts? It might surprise you to find out that some very famous introverts out there have achieved great success and left their mark on the world. The success they achieved came from being able to take what's inside and bring it to the outside, to share it with the world. Extroverts are naturally good at this—they're wired to live outside themselves. Introverts, however, need more internal time. They also need a little understanding of themselves and need to adopt some techniques to move what's inside to the outside.

Studies have shown that introverts account for 25% of the population (you guessed it, extroverts comprise the other 75%). Table 8-1 shows the main characteristics of introverts and extroverts. To be able to interact with the majority, if you're an introvert, you have to learn what your strengths are so you can be heard and fully appreciated. Here are some of the most important strengths introverts have in business.

Table 8-1 Characteristics of Introverts and Extroverts—Which Are You?

Introverts	Extroverts
Recharge by being alone	Energize by contact with others
Prefer to listen	Are talkative
Are thoughtful and reflective	Are action oriented
Focus well	Multitask
Can be mistaken for being aloof	Seen as friendly and outgoing
Need time and space for themselves	Like to surround themselves with others
Keep their thoughts to themselves	Can "think out loud" through talking

Introverts	Extroverts
React internally	React externally
Are quiet	Are expressive
Don't enjoy small talk	Love small talk
Listen first, speak later	Speak first, listen later

Strategy and Organization Come Naturally

Let's say your company wants to be the number one provider of widgets in the country. First, it needs to make production plans; then it needs to establish and send out a sales team, build out its social media channels, and create marketing and public relations plans. When many ideas have to be considered, assimilated, and organized, give this work to an introvert. Introverts like to put puzzles together and make them work in a synergistic way.

An extrovert is often the first person out there shaking hands and making initial connections, but an introvert might need to busily work away at a "master plan" to systematically achieve his or her networking goals. Days might pass before an introvert actually starts making calls. Each approach has its benefits, and neither is wrong. Extroverts can generally build multiple relationships more quickly, which energizes them more and more. Introverts, on the other hand, intuitively know that they have only so much "people energy" available, so they usually create a systematic plan to get the job done.

Problem Solving

Because of their temperament, some introverts can be very intense problem solvers. This intensity is a definite advantage. For instance, introverts process all the pros and cons of a situation, and they intuitively know where the snags will be. This can be a great asset when networking. Whereas an extrovert might be able to offer a variety of possible solutions in a sales call, the introvert is often able to pinpoint the obvious solution on the spot because of his or her ability to solve problems.

I recently benefited from the problem-solving skills of one of my introverted associates. I was telling three clients at lunch about my great fortune in possibly having CNN interview me for an international event. I said that it might be in front of the United Nations building, and while I was talking about it, two of the three people were right there with me, full of energy and enthusiasm.

Then Karen, the head of the department, whom I had noticed was sitting there pensively, quietly asked me, "Have you checked it out with the UN? Do you have all the details from them? Have you considered the insurance issues?" She continued her mental checklist of questions in a very organized manner.

I realized immediately that, no, I hadn't done or even thought about any of these things. I was too excited about the actual happening!

Thank goodness for her detailed, organized, quiet approach. At first I felt as if my bubble had burst. Then I realized that she was right, and her approach and information were going to save me from a lot of headaches and panic. I learned not to get too excited and was saying a silent "thank goodness" that I work with a very organized and processed team whose members made sure that all details were taken care of beforehand.

Good Readers, Good Writers, Good Listeners

Let's say you run a company and want to tap the strength that introverts bring to your staff.

If I want to find out what's going on with one of my introverted business associates, I often ask the person whether he or she is reading any good books. The person usually answers yes. A passionate discussion often follows. Books are the introvert's best friends. Many introverts are very well read and have a broad understanding about a variety of topics. This is due to their natural need for more alone time, and that's exactly what it takes to get through a number of books a year.

If your company is going to a networking event and several large potential clients are going to be there, assign researching these companies to an introvert. The thrill of getting paid to go online to find the latest news on these prospects will almost be too much for the introvert to handle! Have the person put together a mini summary of each potential client for you and the other salespeople, and it will be a great resource for your entire team.

Introverts often feel much more at ease using the written word to communicate their ideas. If they're presented with the option of making a pitch in person or writing a 20-page proposal, the proposal almost always wins. For personal communication, email is often an introvert's best friend. Here introverts can lay out all their ideas clearly and in the exact order they prefer. Writing also allows introverts to nuance their communication, using exact word choices to precisely spell out their thoughts and feelings. Extroverts can also effectively communicate through the written word, but introverts should use this to their advantage in networking. If they can use email communication to get their networking process going, this will give them a great advantage when it comes to making the actual in-person connections.

Your introverted employees' ability to listen could be their greatest asset. Extroverts often find it amazing that introverts can sit and listen to another person for a long time. Extroverts' exuberance naturally makes them want to jump in and make a contribution. However, they often miss or do not share points because there isn't enough time for anyone else to communicate. For introverts, listening comes a little easier. In fact, they might just want to listen and then go back, process the information, and schedule another meeting to talk about solutions. Especially with sensitive clients, introverts can make a great impression with their listening ability. Introverts should know how rare a good listener is, and they should know the difference this makes to the customer. Customers often emotionally embrace their introverted vendors because they feel so cared for when others listen to them.

Dale Carnegie, the grand master of communications skills, always said in his classes that one of the top human relations principles is to let the other person do a great deal of talking—that is, listen to the person! This is music to introverts' ears, for they would rather listen than talk.

Think back to a time when you were at a meeting or event, and as you were introduced to someone, you asked some open-ended questions. What happened? Most likely, the other person started talking and sharing, and you most likely jumped in with other prompter questions. Before you knew it, you were getting ready to leave, and after your exit strategy, the other person probably commented to the host, or at least thought, "I enjoyed talking with you so much. What an interesting person!"

Although you didn't say much, you did do the following:

- Asked open-ended questions
- Paid attention to what the person said
- Showed your interest with your eyes and ears

This is the power of good communication and rapport-building skills. For any cynics reading this and thinking, "That seems manipulative," it is *only* if it's done insincerely. As I always say about anything we discuss in this book, it must be done with the utmost of sincerity, credibility, and character.

EMBRACED OR THE EMBRACER?

Think back to a time when you connected with someone at a business meeting or function.

- Did you approach the other person, or did that person approach you?
- If you were approached, how did it feel?
- What did you think of the embracer?
- How did the conversation go, and who seemed to control it? Or was anyone controlling it?
- If you were the embracer, how did you feel, and what was the reaction of the person you approached?
- How did the conversation go?

In a survey I've conducted at several workshops, I've asked this question after the initial ice breaker exercise in which two people meet and begin a conversation: Who approached whom, and how did it feel?

We've gotten into a lot of discussion about it, and people have overwhelmingly said, "It's a nice feeling to have someone approach or embrace me."

It *is* a nice feeling. Reach out of your comfort zone and make a note to start being the "embracer," or initiator, at the next few meetings, functions, and events you attend. Do this for the next month, and keep track of the results. It could be going into a staff meeting and walking over to greet a colleague from another department, or it could be at your next industry cocktail party where you approach some of the strategic people we talked about previously.

At the end of the month, look at the new contacts and reconnections you made by taking that first step!

Passionate Conversationalists

Now, if you're an introvert, verbal communication might be a challenge. You tend to process your ideas and feelings internally. Extroverts often *need* to verbalize ideas and feelings to get them sorted out. This can be a great advantage for the extrovert, especially in fast-paced environments where answers are needed *now*. However, you, as an introvert, should be encouraged that you can make sure your ideas are heard and considered in a number of ways. When you are passionate and knowledgeable about a given topic and have found a comfortable venue for sharing your views, you can be a quite brilliant communicator and highly effective networker.

Caring

It's hard to say that one temperament style is more caring than another. It's usually a matter of personal choice. The point is that even though introverts might hesitate to share as many of their feelings as their extroverted counterparts, they certainly can care about a situation or business decision just as intensely. When introverts say a few caring words, they have been chosen carefully, and each word has great emotional value attached to it. An introvert might use 10 words to get his or her feelings across to someone, whereas an extrovert might use a hundred words to share the same emotion. Both are valid ways to show emotion and need to be appreciated for their different styles.

If you're an introverted networker, you might want to go the extra mile and send a card or quick email later to reinforce that you truly care about the situation.

Introverts Are Great Networkers

Introverts are quieter by nature, yet they can be great networkers. They just do it differently from the other 75% of the world. The important thing for introverts is to have a networking plan, to provide structure for verbalizing their feelings and ideas most effectively. Introverts' ideas and input are needed; the idea is to work within their own nature. This means being comfortable with the fact that they network differently and have their own style, which might be different from the majority's. Personal marketing and networking are also just as critical for introverts, of course. The key is to grow in the areas you find challenging and to have a toolkit of skills that will help you get your valuable ideas out to the world around you.

Growing Your Introverted Networking Skills

I usually can spot the people who dread coming to my session on networking. How? From the survey I send out in advance. Here are some of the responses I get to the question "What comes to mind when you hear the word *networking*?": "It's selling, and I don't sell." "I'm not good at it—I don't like asking people for things." "It's sleazy." The list goes on, and I can usually pick out these people as soon as I enter the room.

People in the session come to realize that all of us have our own best practices when it comes to networking and personal marketing. However we connect these dots, positive alliances and advocates can help us with what we want to create.

Determine the Areas That Are Most Uncomfortable

What area of networking are you most uncomfortable with? Is it starting conversations? Making small talk? Giving presentations? Cold calling? Think about as many different networking opportunities as you can remember from the past. These can be in business settings, at social events, or at your place of worship. List the top three "I strongly dislike doing" areas of networking. Post them on your computer screen or phone. These are the areas that we're simply going to take some time to learn more about.

Develop a Learning Plan

Now that you have your top three "fear factor" topics of networking, it's time to start turning these into positives in your mind. I'm not saying that you'll ever love doing these things. But you can get to the point that you will no longer avoid these areas, and you'll have these skills in your networking toolkit to use when the time is right.

Make a commitment to do some reading, go to a seminar, or get personal coaching in these areas. Work this into your yearly plan. I suggest giving yourself at least 3 months, and not more than 12, to gradually get some training in these areas. Of course, this depends on how critically you need to get these skills in place. If you're developing a new sales territory and need to increase the business by 400% by next year, then an abbreviated period will have to do. The next step is to start to be purposeful in implementing this learning in your daily work life.

Set Goals for Personal Meetings, Business Parties, and Events

You've become familiar with the three areas of networking you'd like to conquer. I hope the books, articles, webinars, and personal coaching have been helpful and encouraging. You've seen that this is something you can do with a little focused work and effort. Now the challenge is to set some attainable goals that will help you get started using these newfound networking techniques. You want to set goals for personal meetings, business parties, and events.

Often the hardest part is knowing how and where to start. For example, a client of mine, Doug, was overwhelmed. He knew he had to get out in the field and attend new functions and associations. Yet there were so many functions that he could literally go to something every day. I always stress quality versus quantity, and it certainly applies here.

Doug made a list of the top priorities he wanted to get out of the associations he joined. He knew that unless he got involved and went to meetings, it would be a waste of time and money. He started by listing the top 10 organizations from his local chamber of commerce and an industry organization to which his clients belonged.

He used the 2-2-2 strategy (attend two meetings; meet two people and exchange business cards; and arrange two follow-up meetings for breakfast, lunch, or coffee) that we discussed previously. He set a goal of going to at least two meetings of the group, meeting two people, exchanging cards, and arranging two follow-up meetings. Therefore, whether he joined the group or not, he had learned something and had expanded his network by two.

He then narrowed his list to three organizations in which he knew he had a strong interest and whose mission he respected. He carefully cultivated people he knew would like him and got involved in committees to become known in the organization. Over one year, Doug was able to incorporate these three organizations into his life with consistency, ease, and a positive impact.

Write down the associations in which you'd like to invest your time and money to help your career and continued business development. What will be your time commitment each month? What will you do to become known in the group? (*Hint:* Serve on a committee, offer to speak, or write an article for the newsletter.)

With practice, these skills will start to become second nature. The key is to stay focused and committed. Again, we're not talking about changing an introverted nature. We want to gently push ourselves out of our comfort zones, honoring who we are while at the same time stretching beyond ourselves to reach out to others with all that is inside us.

Start in Your Comfort Zone and Work Your Way Out

Who are the people you're most comfortable with? Make a list of family members, friends, and business associates with whom you can establish a networking home base. These people are your comfort zone, so this is where you want to start using your newly developed skills. These people will be the most forgiving when you take some risks and make mistakes. Remember, mistakes are natural. Be easy on yourself. Imagine learning to walk—and soon you'll be running! These people will also give you honest feedback. If the situation is appropriate, you might even tell them about your quest to build up these skills. They will be impressed that you are taking proactive steps to help yourself and still be yourself.

The challenge here is to get out of your comfort zone quickly. When you've had some success networking with those you're comfortable with, it's time to take some bigger risks. The best time to take a risk is when you've had a success. You're at the top of your game, and your confidence is high. Is there a client you've been wanting to call, yet haven't been able to? Now is your time. Go for it! You might not strike gold on the first hit; the goal is to build habits that will make you successful in the long run.

Body Language

As we discussed previously, body language and visual image are 55% of our communication. Introverts need to be especially aware of posture. It's been said that posture is the foundation of your presence. Make sure you look up and stand tall. If you're not in the habit of doing this, it might seem awkward at first. Soon it will become second nature, and you'll see that others find you much more approachable. Then they'll reflect the positive feeling you radiate back to you in their conversation.

Eye Contact

Introverted men should especially be sure to make eye contact. Women, both introverted and extroverted, tend to have less trouble with this. For most men, the tendency is not to relate face to face; side to side is much more comfortable for some. Most of your interpersonal networking will be face to face, though, so make sure you stay focused on the person talking to you. This might not feel completely natural at first, so try to avoid "locking onto" the other person with your eyes. This is where it feels as if someone is trying to drill holes in your head. It's completely normal to look around a bit, yet your attention should always bounce back to the other person's eyes. And remember to look at the "third eye," the space on the forehead right between the eyes.

Creating an Introvert-Friendly Networking Plan

Introverts' networking success can greatly increase with a plan. As I mentioned earlier, this will come easily for most introverts, with their organizing and strategizing temperament. Everyone's plan is different.

Here I have attempted to give you some ideas that you can incorporate into your own personal plan, if you're an introvert. The important part of the plan is to maximize your strengths, yet stretch yourself in areas that tend to not come as naturally. Consistency will be your best friend in following your plan. I recommend that you ask the following questions in making your networking plan:

- "What is my ultimate goal for networking? Is it finding new business? Developing current accounts? Becoming known in my industry or in one that I serve? Building a stronger internal team and developing new alliances? What are my personal strengths as an introvert, and how can I maximize these in networking toward my goal? Are they organizational skills, writing skills, or problem-solving skills?"

- "What is my strategy for blending my strengths in areas in which I need to stretch? How much time will I spend networking using social media and electronic communication? How much time will I spend networking on the phone? Do I have goals for myself in this? How much time will I spend networking in person? Again, what are my goals for these types of events? How can I stretch myself in this and also honor who I am as an introvert?"

- "How can I integrate all forms of networking into a system that will work for what I do? Will I use an opener letter before I call my contact? When appropriate, will I always try to get an in-person appointment when I am networking over the telephone? How can I integrate my organizational strengths to be more prepared for when I am in a person-to-person situation? How might I use my writing strengths to add to what I present in person?"

- "What books and educational or coaching resources might I tap to continue to sharpen the areas in which I am strong while not neglecting the areas that challenge me? Do I have a yearly schedule for this? Have I set some goals on reading articles or books that will help me improve this year?"

- "Do I need to include in my plan regular reminders about areas of personal development, such as making eye contact, having good posture, using proper etiquette, and/or developing character?"

Let's walk through some of the ways you can maximize your introverted temperament to develop new business and build your networking skills.

Maximizing Your Writing Strengths

If you're in a fast-paced or highly interactive environment, you'll want to conserve your social energy, to avoid being tapped out when you really need it. One technique that can work well for introverted networkers is maximizing the amount of written communication in their networking approach. A caution up front: The idea is to maximize this strength, yet not totally rely on the computer and social media, because it might be more comfortable than being face to face or talking on the phone with people. You'll still need to be personally out there as much as possible. Nothing takes the place of an in-person meeting.

Writing for Publications and the Web

Introverts can maximize their networking effectiveness by raising their profiles by writing articles for magazines, newsletters, and newspapers; guest posting on blogs; and posting on social media sites.

When I'm looking through industry e-zines, I often see if they take contributed articles. If it looks like they do, I email or call the editors to see if they're interested in an article. As they tell you about the topics they might be covering in upcoming issues, you might say that you'd like to send a one-paragraph proposal for an article you could write. Or if you have an idea right there on the phone that you can really write about with proficiency, pitch it and see what they have to say.

If they don't need an article at that time, let them know that you'd like to send them a letter with your information, in case they ever need to interview someone in your field. I usually include a short, casual letter thanking them for their time and offering my time as a resource in case they need someone to talk about something in their industry. I might also include an article I've written or other articles for which I have been interviewed. If I think there's some potential with the publication, I add it to my follow-up plan and find ways to keep in contact periodically.

It's often easier to get published on the web than it is in print. My articles usually run on a magazine or trade organization's e-zine, and I track them with Google Alerts. And remember to thank all for the connections you make. This is part of the thank you chain I introduce in the next part of the book; it works well and should be a consistent part of the plan.

Put your articles on your own website, tweet them, and, in some cases, post them on Facebook. You might have to make them less industry specific to reach a more general audience, and this is easy to do. In fact, it's possible to change the same article to fit a wide variety of industries. Remember, the material is fresh to the accountants, even if you already used it in the cosmetic industry. Just make sure you take the time to research each industry and customize your article using industry-specific language and phrases.

Another up-and-coming way to get your name out using the written word is to capitalize on the current fascination with blogs. What is a blog? A blog, short for *weblog*, is basically a diary or log of your thoughts about a particular topic that's posted on the Web for the whole world to see. Blogs are especially useful if you deal with cutting-edge news. For instance, if you're a political consultant, people can go to your blog and see if you have anything in there on the President's new initiative to reform Social Security. If you're an expert in your industry, or even if you're not, you can start a blog to get your thoughts out to see what people think. From there, you can set up a chat room for them to respond to your thoughts, or they can simply email you if they would like to talk further. This can be a great way to make contacts on the Web. If your blog is particularly good, people will start to add it to the Links page of their websites. Soon you can become the "expert" in your particular area of interest as the momentum of your blog grows on the Web. Today everyone is an author and has a blog—find a way to make yours stand out.

Online Networking Communities

Online communities are where *you* have to be. The enormous opportunities made available by all online communities could take a book to explain. Be sure you have a LinkedIn presence, set up a Twitter account, and know about Facebook; when appropriate, set up a business fan page. Be sure to post on LinkedIn groups, and ask and answer questions to gain visibility and get known for your expertise and knowledge.

Please go ahead and post it. This can often open up a conversation online and then lead to face-to-face discussions. I am always an advocate of real live people getting together face to face—there's no greater form of communication. Try what's comfortable for you—it will be a great way to meet people.

Social Media Networking

Introverted people tend to agree that online they become "online extroverts." The same people who say it's challenging to introduce themselves in a room full of people feel at ease striking up a conversation on LinkedIn, Twitter, or Facebook. The whole awkward feeling seems to be removed.

This is the best foot in the door; however, as with anything, use these vehicles wisely. They're tools for our interpersonal communication. Make every interaction personal. My biggest pet peeve is getting LinkedIn invitations that just have the default message to link in. Take the time to say something to introduce yourself for either connecting or reconnecting. I do this with each invitation I send out and then do the same when I reply. Make the message personal—for example, I might use, "Great to link in from Andrea Nierenberg" in the subject line and then add a line or two on something that I read from the person's profile. Your response rate will rise dramatically.

I do send out a monthly tip-of-the-month e-zine that often gets forwarded throughout a company. And to a variety of people, this has been a great way for an introvert like me to also start to connect with people I might not have otherwise met.

With every reply you get, send a personal note of thanks, no matter what. The idea is to get the conversation started, not close the deal. You might just follow up with someone you'd like to get to know because you saw the person mentioned in the newspaper or trade journal, heard about his or her recent success, or thought the person could benefit from a product or service you offer. You might have seen it on LinkedIn, Google Alerts, or any material that arrives in your inbox. You might not always get a response, but that's okay.

The next step is to get on the phone and talk with the person. Then at least you have an opener: "I'm following up on the email I sent you about such and such." Usually the response is positive, such as, "Oh, I was meaning to get back to you...." You might even put in your email that you'll follow up via phone, if that's appropriate—better yet, ask for the person's preferred method of communication for next steps. Again, the goal is to find common ground and eventually have a chance to talk with others face to face if you can really help them with a need, be a resource, or learn something from each other.

Opener Letters

Another technique to get things started is to use the opener letter. After I've determined whom I want to contact, I try to figure out how to customize an email that might open some doors when I call the person to follow up. Usually I try to work one type of business or industry at a time. For example, one month I concentrate on my prospects in the legal profession. During the following months, I might focus on real estate, cosmetics, and fashion and ad agencies, in that order. As I work on each industry, I do my best to follow its current trends by reading online blogs, journals, association newsletters, and, of course, Google Alerts that are specific to that industry. I do this between appointments or while traveling. When I know I'll be writing my opener letter for a particular industry, I make sure to take written and mental notes as I do my reading.

Does a current trend make it possible for me to help people in an industry improve their communication skills in some way? Even new legislation that might affect a particular industry could provide a lead on where my services are needed. The most effective way to write the opener letter is to know what's going on in the particular companies you're writing to. When I'm writing to an industry for the first time, I research only the top 10 companies I want to reach out to. This usually gives me a good idea of what might be happening in all the companies I'm writing to. The key is not to pretend you are *the* expert in your letter—just show them that you're informed and ready to let them know how you can be of genuine service to them. We have so much online research at our fingertips—we all expect people who connect with us to be totally informed. As introverts, we know this is key in our communication.

No formula dictates how to write an opener letter, although you might find some samples or examples on the Internet. The basic letter has an introduction, a body, and a conclusion or point of action you'd like the recipient to take. Take some time to introduce yourself, point to your product or service, and identify how you think you might be able to work together. In the body, you might include some industry-specific details that grab the reader's attention, along with possible solutions that you could provide. In the closing, let the recipient know that you will follow up on the phone, and give a specific time frame for when you will be doing this. Then make sure you follow up within that time. This formula works also when you're reaching out for an exploratory interview or even when you're connecting with someone within your global firm. The template and basic formula are the same—what you put in will be unique and yours alone.

By the way, you can also add a postscript to the letter. People often skip down to the P.S. to see what the email or letter is about, without reading the whole thing. The idea is to capture your main idea and reiterate it in one or two sentences. For example: "P.S. Please remember, I'm offering a free consultation this month on how the art and science of networking can help you find, grow, and keep the best business relationships."

Using a Script

When you do get someone on the phone, ask whether the person received your letter. If not, or if the person hasn't gotten to it yet, have a script ready to keep you from stumbling. Go through in your head all the different answers you anticipate, from "Yes" to "I'm too busy right now," and have some idea of what you will say to each response.

You might have a few questions ready about the firm or some interesting ways others in the industry have benefited from your product or service. If the person can't talk at the moment, which is usually the case, ask when you can follow up. Be prepared that, 99% of the time, you will go right into voicemail, so think in advance with your script what you will say that will give the recipient a reason to listen and take your next call and correspondence. Remember to be as gracious as possible; we all have gotten calls from people at the wrong time. Put yourself in the other person's shoes. Above all, be friendly, courteous, and respectful. The person might be busy now, and later when you call, when the person needs something you have, he or she will probably show a much warmer side.

POST IT AND PRACTICE

Be prepared, write a script, and practice. I call it P.O.S.T.

P	Prepare your script in advance.
O	Organize your thoughts and what you want to say. Less is more.
S	Succeed with your own system.
T	Take your time.

Follow-Up

Follow-up is key. As I like to say, after all is said and done, much more is said than done. Email your follow-up immediately. Make sure you email a week before your meet-up, to make contact, and then contact the person again the day before the meeting, to confirm. Email articles from LinkedIn and all the different sites and information you receive. Always send a follow-up email thanking the person for the time he or she did give you. Then, while your call is still fresh in the person's mind, elaborate briefly—only one paragraph, at most—on why you were calling and what action you would like to take with the person. You might ask for more information about how the person selects vendors or internal partners, or what the person does when he or she needs a custom solution in the area in which you specialize.

Person to Person

Person-to-person connecting can often be the hardest area for the introvert. However, whether you are an accountant, dentist, author, or artist, personal marketing is the key to giving what you have to give to a world that needs it. Personal marketing is about putting your best foot forward in front of other people.

I've already mentioned many of the challenges and strengths you possess as an introvert. You're known in your field for your expertise through your written articles and personal publicity. You've maximized your introvert traits by using social media to make good contacts. You've done your phone work, and now here you are, face to face with your contact. Perhaps this is a sales presentation, a "meet and greet" where your company comes in and does a presentation on your products or services, or a networking event where, by "chance," you've run into your contact. Regardless, now is the time to really connect with others in the most personal of ways, face to face.

The important point is to be yourself. That's right—you can only be one person, and that's yourself! Just put your best foot forward and let those ideas and goals come out; you'll be surprised at how positive a response you get from others when they see your passion for what you are doing. Remember, you do have good ideas and want to help people where you can. You're a giver, and you want the opportunity to learn and to serve. You are naturally the internalizer. Your gift is to process situations and challenges from within and create new paradigms for the outside world to use. Even though introverts make up 25% to 35% of the population, the other 75% of the population needs what you can contribute. Let them know who you are and what you can offer, and I believe you'll eventually see all your thoughts and dreams come to life.

Even if the people you meet aren't an exact match for what you do in business, focus on them and learn something from them. You might have to politely break conversation and move on in your networking, yet you'll have connected with the person and feel good about it. This respectful treatment of others will come back to you in many ways. Believe me, as I've told the story before, when I, an introvert, first came to New York City after graduating from college years ago, I knew no one. Now I have many colleagues, clients, connections, and friends in every realm of life and business. Your network takes time to build and is continually growing, and I am richer in my experiences for it.

Small Talk for Introverts

The biggest challenge for most introverts in face-to-face communication is small talk. Small talk is simply the social lubricant that gets conversations started.

You've probably been in group discussions where the speaker comes up with an icebreaker to get people talking. This is all small talk; only it's in the context of two individuals instead of a group. Some introverts think there's something wrong or less than honest in making small talk. This need not be the case. You can make small talk with people while holding on to your integrity. Just be honest when you speak and respectfully withhold your opinion if you disagree. Most people won't press you too hard to agree with them when you're first getting to know them. If they do and you're uncomfortable, simply excuse yourself politely and find someone else to talk with. This will apply to maybe 1% of the people you run into; the other 99% will be just as eager as you are to make good connections and learn something along the way.

Of course, some practical tips are especially helpful for the introverted networker. Earlier, I mentioned using a script. This can be a huge help for the quieter networker and will give you something to get the conversation started. For the introvert, I also suggest having a few questions or comments ready as conversation starters. Extroverts tend to have an easier time finding things to talk about. Introverts will want to map these out in their head beforehand. Consider this example of a mental list:

- Ask what others thought of the speaker tonight.

- Ask why they came to this particular event.

- Ask how this event compares to other, similar events they've been to.

Remember that 75% of the people you talk to love to talk. All you have to do is ask a few questions, and the conversation will flow on and on—and they'll walk away thinking you're a brilliant conversationalist. And the fact is, because you're such a good listener, you are! And you will have learned some new things along the way. Listening is the key ingredient to great networking, and introverts, as a whole, do this with almost perfection.

Of course, be ready with your 30-second introduction when other people ask you about yourself. If you sense they're truly interested in what you're saying, be bold and let them see your passion, whatever it might be. This can be a great way to go from the small talk stage to really forming a personal relationship with someone. And remember the four must-do's: Learn something, give something, take something, and find a way to follow up.

Partnering with Extroverts

One way to capitalize on the natural skills of quieter networkers is to encourage them to work with extroverts who will naturally be good at making introductions and getting the conversation going. While this is happening, your introvert has picked up on the mood of each person, has analyzed the potential for doing business, and is thinking about how he or she can solve the potential customer's problem. The introverted executive has probably also figured out the personality style of the prospect or new connection. When the conversation naturally reaches the point where a solution is needed, it's time for the introvert to take the stage. The extrovert will need to defer to the introvert as the "expert" and move out of the way. This is especially effective at business events when engaging companies that you'd like to do business with yet have never interacted with.

Tag-Team Sales Call

Back from a sales call, Steve and Bill had totally different takes on what happened. Steve, the extrovert, walked into the manager's office saying, "What a great call! We aced it! They're definitely going to go forward with the proposal." Bill, on the other hand, looked puzzled as he expressed the opposite point of view and scratched his head in bewilderment. He was thinking, "Did I actually just participate in the same meeting Steve did?" Of course he did—what happened was that these two people looked at the meeting in completely different ways.

When Steve was telling the client, Rochelle, all about their suggested proposal, he was talking without listening as much and wasn't paying attention to details or body language. He was focused only on what he was saying, not on the nonverbal gaze he was getting from Rochelle. Bill, on the other hand, paid close attention to Rochelle and saw how she stiffened every time Steve blurted out another claim about why their product was the best and why they had to move forward. Bill watched her get interrupted if she tried to speak until she finally sat in total silence waiting for the meeting to end. Because her style was also that of the introvert, she smiled and said "Thank you." As she ushered them to the door, she said she'd think about it and that she had to dash off to another meeting.

Steve interpreted the meeting as a definite sale, where Bill saw it as a definite no-go. What could each of them have done differently to help the other and create a winning situation? Steve needed to carry his intangible toolkit—he needed to bring his ears and eyes. If he had observed Rochelle's body language, stopped talking, and started listening, he could have asked open-ended, high-gain questions.

Bill, on the other hand, with his strong intuitive and detail skills, saw what was happening. If he could have jumped in at the appropriate time to save his colleague by asking a question or giving a fact based on the research he had done before the meeting, he could have turned the meeting around. He was totally organized before he left the office and had a script in place, complete with potential objections and answers.

Steve and Bill needed to prepare before the meeting, go over the possible scenarios to decide what to do, and look at the situation from both vantage points. "Tag-team" meetings with opposite personalities can produce amazing results. Each person sees the situation differently; with some preparation and time management, together they can work wonders.

Look at your own situation; then go to your next meeting with one of your extroverted colleagues and plan in advance. Write down and discuss your strengths and areas in which each of you is challenged. After the meeting, debrief what did or didn't happen and how you can move forward and learn from each other.

Recharging for Introverts

You might be thinking that all this talk about personal marketing is starting to wear you out. That's okay! It's just the way introverts are wired. Introverts need to take time to recharge and not feel guilty. Remember, you're processing things at a much deeper level than most people do. This is your strength, but it's also a great challenge because you need the time to disengage from your external environment to give your internal self time to think, resolve, and rest.

The lunch meeting can be a great time to get business done. I recommend using mealtimes as often as possible to get to know people. This is one way we humans really connect with each other—by eating together. "Let's get a coffee" is also a very effective way to take things from the purely business to a more personal level. However, if you're an introvert, you need to plan some time for yourself throughout the day, if possible. If you can do this over lunch with a good book or when watching a webinar or catching up on emails, great! If you need to use your lunches to conduct business, then I strongly suggest taking a couple 10-minute breaks in the morning and afternoon to recharge. This can be spent simply by reading an e-zine, going for a quick walk, or even taking a short power nap (5 minutes—I don't want you getting fired for napping at work)! Many firms, like Google and Facebook, have created relaxation rooms for their employees to decompress and regain energy and creativity. You might not think you have the time to do these things, yet in the end, you'll get more done every day by keeping yourself recharged.

Quiet, Yet Quite Successful

As I have tried to stress, in many ways, introverts rule. They make excellent networkers and engage in their own powerful and strategic way. Their natural ability to process things internally and their great listening skills make them valuable assets to any team or business, especially when teamed with extroverts who know and value their abilities.

Introverts' intrinsic desire to have things organized and to formulate a plan often sets them apart from the crowd. In time, it makes them very successful at whatever they set out to do. For many introverts, writing is a hidden talent they need to take advantage of. Writing lists for assignments, writing names of various contacts, and devising a networking plan are all safe and comfortable activities for introverts. Then they can sit down by themselves, review the lists, and evaluate their next steps in connecting with people face to face. Remember to use your internal passion to your advantage in person-to-person conversations. People love to talk with someone who's passionate about something they're also passionate about. Always stretch yourself, while honoring who you are, and take a break now and again to recharge. That way, you'll be your best for yourself and for your client.

TWO GREAT NETWORKERS, TWO DIFFERENT STYLES

When I visited my lifelong friends Trudy and Bill, who are also my godparents, I was reminded again of the networking strengths of both extroverts and introverts. Trudy meets and greets, talks, and acts friendly to everyone. She's also the first to stand up and give a short speech. Bill, conversely, would be content to hold a conversation with just a few people. He sometimes looked as if he was holding court when people gathered around him waiting to hear what he would say, because anything he said was important. He was intelligent and articulate. Together they were a powerful couple and both superb networkers, yet each would say, "I'm not a networker; I'm just being who I am." Of course, this is the key. They both have superb interpersonal skills that have brought them a lifetime of friends and contacts. At this writing, Trudy and Bill were married 68 years, and she's still going strong at 93!

Consider these six ways introverts can get networking results:

1. Take quiet time. It's your time to restore and recharge, and often creativity emerges.

2. Prepare. Work ahead of time to lay out the steps for the results you want to achieve.

3. Listen closely. Utilize your strengths as an engaged listener, and be totally focused.

4. Have a focused conversation. This combines listening and purposeful talking.

5. Write. Think, process, compose, and create.

6. Use social media thoughtfully and purposefully through the channels of LinkedIn, Facebook, Twitter, YouTube, and everything else emerging daily. Start by taking 10 to 15 minutes a day to network through social media and see what develops over time. Focus on a few sites only—don't spread yourself too thin.

These need to be your networking "I am" statements—and keep adding to this list.

- I am prepared and focused.

- I am a good listener.

- I am approachable.

- I am interested in others and what they have to say.

- I am someone whom others trust.

- I AM....

In the next chapter, we focus on how to use follow-up to make your network really thrive.

Exercise: Networking Self-Test for Introverts

1. When is the best time to think of networking?

   _____

   _____

2. What is the mistake people most often make in the way they define or describe networking or personal marketing?

   _____

   _____

3. What are the three top things you want to learn about every person you meet?

   _____

   _____

4. When you meet someone, what two things can you do to build rapport and trust?

   _____

   _____

5. What is one thing you can do to inject some small talk into your conversations?

_____

_____

6. What can you do to be totally prepared for every networking encounter, to make each one totally comfortable?

_____

_____

7. How do you continually work on your introduction and get to know your questions and exit strategies according to your own organized plan?

_____

_____

8. How many people would you consider to be true advocates who could explain what you do and who you are to someone else in less than 30 seconds?

_____

_____

9. How do you want to be remembered when you meet someone, and what's your approach?

_____

_____

10. What are you going to do starting today and every day to keep your network alive, growing, and building for you?

_____

_____

9

Follow-up: A Road Map for Growth

"Avoid shortcuts. They always take too much time in the long run."
–Anonymous

After any event, as I'm walking out, I have my exit strategy in place for building my network. I'm ready to input information about new people I've met into my contact database, write follow-up notes, email any articles I've promised, and get the contact information of at least two people to set up meetings with. I might be masterful at working the room and making contacts (though introverts and extroverts do it differently), but without follow-up, one thing is certain: Nothing will ever happen.

I repeatedly hear people say, "I was going to follow up, but I got so busy!" or "I wasn't sure if the contact I made really meant for me to contact him." Whatever the excuse, if I've learned anything about finding, growing, and keeping contacts, it's that follow-up is the key to growing your network and your business. What I remember has a way of being rewarded over time.

"Must-Do's" After a Meeting

After any event or meeting, you have a number of opportunities to follow up quickly and efficiently, based on conversations you had and contacts you made. Timing is of the essence. Tomorrow you will only have more things to do and more excuses for not doing it, so do it now.

At least 24 hours after a meeting, send a note or email, or call to say any of the following, depending on the circumstances of your meeting:

- **"It was nice to meet you."** I attended an association dinner where one of the guests, Nick, was sharing some information about his company. Even though we met and chatted only as we were walking out the door, I sent him a note the following day telling him how much I had enjoyed meeting him and hearing his presentation. He responded, and we met several times over the years. I now work with his company as a client. He refers me all the time, and we've had many collaborations. We've also formed a great friendship. It never would have happened without follow-up.

- **"Thank you for your time and consideration."** Anyone who knows me or has heard my advice knows that I strongly believe in the power of the handwritten note. Here's how the power of a note can work: After a long day of meetings and interviews with the partners of a company where I was presenting a proposal for management coaching, I left armed with my note cards. Two days later, everyone received a personal note from me, thanking him or her for taking the time to meet with me. As it turned out, I didn't get the project and was told I was a "close second." So I sent each of them another note, this time email or text, depending on their preferred method of communication. I wrote "Thank you for your time and consideration" and expressed my hope that our paths might cross again. Some people might think that was a lot of work because I didn't get to close the deal. Yet it paid off, because a couple months later, I was called back in to do a more extensive project with some of the organization's internal people and created a strategic alliance to work with some of its clients. You never know how your thank you notes will work. The personal note tells the client or prospect that you took the time to write, which will make you stand out. If you say that your handwriting isn't good, I have two options for you: Either print or utilize a great system that I also use (see my website, www.appreciationpower.com).

- **"Perhaps we can meet again."** When I speak with people, I always ask how it might be best to follow up. Remember, at various networking events, your goal is to establish rapport and ask for permission to meet again. This was the case when I attended a huge industry event not long ago. I started chatting with the woman sitting to my left at lunch. Shortly into our conversation, it was time for the program to begin, and she had to dash out. She didn't have her card, so I wrote down her name and her company; then I went to the company website and emailed her the next day, suggesting we meet for breakfast the following week. We did. I was able to hook her up with a new supplier, and she is now a new contact for me. Find opportunities to pay it forward.

- **"Thank you for the useful information."** I always practice this suggestion—and it's also nice to be on the receiving end! Recently, I received several nice notes and emails after giving a short presentation at an event. I remember one, in particular, that came to my email box the next day, with the subject line, "Thank you for sharing some helpful thoughts." I always remember the people who follow up with me to say thanks or tell me that my information was helpful. We all like to hear this. Take the time today to think about someone who has recently given you some useful information—whether the person is an existing contact or someone you met recently—and drop him or her a note or email to say so. Doing these follow-ups is more than courteous; it distinguishes you from the other people your contact has met. You will differentiate yourself.

If you've promised to send materials, call to set up a meeting, or pass on a referral, keep your word and do it within the time promised—or sooner. It's easy to make these promises at a meeting or event, but a person who follows up in a timely manner is remembered and trusted.

Call within two weeks after suggesting a get-together, whether over a meal or at a more formal meeting. "Let's do lunch" is just an old cliché, unless you make it happen. And we have many times in the day to meet for a meal or snack or drink. Suggest it only if you mean it, and then follow up to set a specific date and place. And remember to call or send an email to confirm the day before. Things happen in life, and people appreciate it when you take the time to do this added courtesy. If they must cancel, you'll have an opportunity to make other plans. Either way, you come across as being sincere and professional.

When a contact provides you with a referral or offers to pass on your information to help you, be sure to say thank you and keep your contact in the loop by letting him or her know the results, whatever happens. The same holds true for any tangible advice you get from a contact. People who offer to help you, and then go out of their way to do it, deserve to know the results of their advice. And they certainly deserve a thank you! Again, these people are some of your advocates—they are helping to market you, and I consider them my "clients," too.

Several months ago, when I spoke to a group about this subject, Jane, who had invited me, said, "Andrea, I must share a story, because as you are explaining the importance of this simple courtesy, I am seething with anger regarding a recent situation." She told me that her husband had referred their friend, Bill, for a project at her husband's client's company. They heard nothing from Bill until several months later at a party, when a mutual acquaintance told them that Bill had gotten the project. Never once had Bill thanked them for the referral, let them know how the project was going, or even had the courtesy to let them know he'd been successful. Jane was angry about Bill's rudeness after her husband had gone out of his way to help him. Some weeks later, she called me to say that Bill had recently left a message on her husband's machine asking if he could help out a "friend"—yet there was still no thank you! Needless to say, no further help was offered.

You've probably been in situations like this when people forget their most important client, advocate, or referral source. Be sure to avoid those kinds of mistakes, and take the time right now to repair any inadvertent damage you might have done. Usually it's an innocent mistake—we simply forget. Dig deep and go back through your entire database. This is a useful and helpful exercise.

Doing these follow-ups is good manners, helps build solid relationships for the future, and shows respect for others. *Respect* is the key word here. Remember, people do business with those whom they know and respect. They will want to help you again when the opportunity arises.

AFTER YOUR FIRST MEETING

A gentle touch is often required as a follow-up with people we have just met. First and foremost, take the time to build rapport. If you've met someone new and then the next day you ask to set up a sales call or ask for a referral, you risk coming across as aggressive and self-centered, and you could damage a developing relationship. Remember to ask for permission to stay in touch. Send a note first, saying how much you enjoyed meeting the person and suggesting another meeting.

As I was waiting for my dinner guest one night at a restaurant, the woman in the next booth and I struck up a conversation. It turned out she had been a speaker at an event I had attended. The world is small. I'd thought she was very interesting and insightful. I began discussing a few of the things I remembered from her talk, and we were still talking when our respective dinner partners arrived. I sent her a note the following day, along with a copy of my first book. She called me soon afterward and invited me to give a speech for her organization. Follow up! These serendipitous opportunities happen all the time when we are open and aware.

Thank You Notes

As I have said, one of the best follow-up techniques is a simple thank you note. It seems so obvious to thank someone, yet many people fail to do so. A handwritten note clearly makes you stand out and separates you from the others. At the very least, send off an email or pick up the phone after your meeting just to say thanks, or send a text—you'll begin to build a relationship. I remember this from several years ago when I sent a new contact a handwritten note. He responded to me by saying, "I know I shouldn't have been surprised, yet in this day and age of everything electronic, your note certainly made an impact." I still remember this—and it was five years ago. Now a handwritten note makes even more of an impact in our electronic world.

Eight reasons to send a thank you note follow:

1. **For time and consideration:** This is one of the four "must do's" after a meeting. It also applies to many other situations, such as interviews, one-on-one meetings, and social encounters.

2. **For a compliment you received:** I met a woman at an event who had one of the most amazing pens I've ever seen. It was a great conversation starter. She told me it was her "signature piece," and she loved it. I later sent her an article that I saw on pens, and she sent me a note written with her special pen thanking me for the compliment!

3. **For a piece of advice given:** A client called me to offer her advice on how to design an upcoming presentation for some decision makers in her company. She spent quite a bit of time with me, so I immediately sat down and wrote her a thank you note for her time and help.

4. **For business:** This is a "must do"! Every time someone does business with you or gives you an order, drop the person a thank you note. Remember, someone else could have gotten that business instead of you. Remember also to send a thank you note to all those who were responsible for making the decision. Too often people thank only the top person; however, most decisions are made with input from many people. Be sure to send a note to everyone who was part of the decision. This will show your appreciation and reinforce your name with others in your client's business. It also strengthens what I call "surrounding the account," where you expose your potential client to your name and business on as many fronts as possible.

5. **For a referral:** After I spoke at a real estate company, one of the agents in the audience referred me to one of his clients. I sent him a note immediately. He continually tells me how much he appreciated that simple note. When you thank in writing the people who go out of their way for you, it guarantees you will stay on their radar screen. It shows you took the time.

6. **For a gift:** I read a wonderful story about a little girl who learned the power of thank you notes when she was only 7. She thanked her mom and grandmother for every gift she received, often with a little drawing or card. Once she was so excited about the unique toothbrush her grandma had given her that she wrote up a little

note saying she would think of her grandma every night when she brushed her teeth with her new toothbrush! You might be smiling—this kid is bright. Who do you think is remembered and rewarded all the time?

7. **For help on a project:** I think of all the great people on my virtual team who continually help me with my projects. My assistant, Linda, is always there to proof, and I always know my work will look great. Margie, Scott, and John are always helping me by adding their wonderful expertise. Even though we've worked together for years, I always send notes and delicious brownies to show my appreciation.

8. **Even when you're "rejected":** The door is never shut. My mantra is, always thank people for their time and consideration, even if nothing comes of it—because sometimes it does! And you can always learn something. One of my clients told me how her rejection of a consultant turned into an offer. When the first candidate she chose for the project didn't work out, she looked again at the other possibilities. She recalled one consultant who had sent a note thanking her for her consideration, despite the rejection letter he got. She called him in for another meeting and subsequently hired him for the project.

THANK YOU NOTES PAY OFF

Recently, I found out that Dave, a former client of mine, had left his company to pursue another passion. I sent him a note, thanking him for all his help in coordinating our projects and making my work so easy at his company. I also sent thank you notes to the senior people with whom Dave used to work, in addition to his former assistant. Over the next two months, there was a flurry of activity at the company. I came up on the radar screens of all the people I'd contacted, which came from my note to each of them. As you can see, it's important to take the time to write these notes—they'll pay off over time.

My Thank You Chain

I've mentioned my thank you chain before and said that I often use it to thank everyone who has helped me along the way. It's a simple, efficient, and powerful way to follow up and be remembered. I have thank you chains throughout many companies where I work. For instance, I was giving a speech at an association meeting and met three new people who hired me for projects. The first thank you went to the organizer of the association meeting, and the others went to all the people I knew from the group. I also sent over a basket of goodies because, without them, I never would have met these people. I have done several projects at one of the companies and continue to thank my original and secondary contacts so the thank you chain can grow.

I even have a system for my thank you chain. I track every single opportunity back to the first introduction. I put this information into my database so that I can easily go back and see how the connection began. I thank all the people in my chain by phone, email, text, social media, or note, depending on their preferred method of communication. People are often surprised by my thank you because they might not have realized the part they played in the chain. It's fun to tell them how it evolved and that, if it hadn't been for them, I wouldn't have had this success. And I thank them! This suggestion is both simple and powerful.

YOUR PERSONAL THANK YOU CHAIN

Working from present to past, think about the chain of events and people who led you to your current job (business, profession, or a major client). Make a list of the people who helped you through referrals or in other ways. Write, call, or send each of them an email to thank them. Start by asking yourself:

- How did I get my current job?

- How did I get into this industry?

- How did I meet my last two major clients?

THE POWER OF NINE

Every day, I go through my database and do the following:

1. Send three handwritten notes.

2. Send three additional emails or texts.

3. Make three additional phone calls.

4. Bonus: I link in with someone daily.

My database includes people's names and their preferred means of communication (*E* for email, *V* for voicemail, *T* for text, and *L* for LinkedIn) so that I can say thank you or just touch base in the way and system they prefer. When combined with my personal notes, this becomes a powerful and effective way to maintain meaningful business relationships. It takes only about 16 minutes of your day, and it's very "net worth it"!

Building Trust

People do business with those they trust and respect. *Trust* is the key word, and building trust takes time and patience. When we network, we need to learn to respect others' timetables. Often new contacts don't respond in a timely fashion—at least, it seems that way. They may be busy with their own deadlines and have many responsibilities that keep them from responding to you immediately. So how can we move the process forward without "pushing" other people too hard, which will only make them more reluctant? If someone you've met doesn't call back after being given a great introduction or offer, avoid being seen as a pest. Life is busy and challenging, and we never know what is going on in someone else's life. Stay the course, touch base periodically, and see if something develops over time. Take the high road—there's always less traffic there.

When you do connect, ask a few productive questions for your follow-up. "How do you and your organization prefer to learn about new suppliers or external partners?" or "What is the best way to present product information to you?" This way, you make it easy to do business with you, and you ultimately receive the response you're looking for.

Rushing a communication—hurrying off the phone or sending an email that's not carefully written—can be another networking stumbling block. It tells the new contact that you're trying to move through the process in a cold and mechanical way. Even when we have long lists of people to contact, it takes very little effort to develop a personalized approach. Here are three ways to do it:

1. Ask your contacts how they want the issue to be handled and how they prefer to communicate. Some people prefer that everything be done in writing; others would rather receive a quick follow-up phone call or email letting them know about new opportunities that can benefit them. This is so simple. For example, many of your calls might elicit no response. However, when you email, text, or send something through LinkedIn, the response is immediate. You have just learned to communicate with people the way they like.

2. Check on new contacts regularly. Have your follow-up plan in place. Mark your calendar for the next significant date on your contact's calendar. Connect by phone or electronically before sending new information and say that you hope to connect with him or her at an upcoming conference or meeting.

3. Develop a networking game plan. New contacts will never develop into anything important unless you have a long-term plan in place for keeping in touch with them. Keep a readily available list of all contacts. Using that list, develop a plan that is appropriate for all the contacts, and choose which ones should receive special treatment. For instance, you might see that an effective follow-up strategy with a key contact could be looking for him or her at an upcoming business function. Another contact might appreciate a note with helpful information. When you find out which method is most effective with each of your contacts, build on what works and develop the skills you need, such as writing and speaking, to make meaningful connections with those people. Look at the client/contact profile and see how much you learn about people as you get to know them over time.

Remember that the true key to growing your network is follow-up. Now that you have an expanding network, you need to figure out how to keep it alive. In the next chapters, we check out some great strategies for staying in touch with your contacts. Before you move on, try these quick exercises to help you follow up and grow your network.

Exercise 1: Eight Ways to Say "Thank You"

Look at the following eight reasons for sending a thank you note. Next to each reason, write down at least one name of someone to whom you can write a thank you note this week.

1. For time and consideration _____

2. For a compliment you received _____

3. For a piece of advice given _____

4. For business _____

5. For a referral _____

6. For a gift _____

7. For help on a project _____

8. Even when you're "rejected" _____

Exercise 2: Other Notes

Other types of notes you can send anytime to stay in touch and be helpful. Write down at least one name of someone to whom you can write a note this week. Consider the following reasons:

1. FYI (for your information) _____

2. Congratulations _____

3. Nice talking to (or meeting) you _____

4. Thinking of you _____

5. Other _____

Exercise 3: Who Will You Help?

Think of people in your network whom you can help or provide with a connection, information, or a referral. Write down their names and take action.

1. _____

2. _____

3. _____

T   Take the time to say thank you to someone.

H   Have a plan of action to incorporate this strategy every day.

A   Articulate your note or compliment with powerful language.

N   Notice something special about each person.

K   Keep in touch sincerely and in your own style.

Y   *You* is the most important word when thanking someone; tell others what is special about them.

O   Organize yourself so that this process becomes seamless.

U   Understand the power of a sincere and considerate thank you.

"Life is like a soap opera. God is the head writer, your story line keeps changing, it's a daily event, and there are Friday cliffhangers."
—Anonymous

Appendix

Characteristics of a Good Listener

On a scale of 1–5, with 5 being the highest, fill in the blank to indicate the degree to which you already practice these positive listening behaviors. Go through the list twice, first rating yourself with the person you listen to the best and then rating yourself with the person to whom you find it most difficult to listen.

Best	Worst	
_____	_____	I make regular eye contact with the speaker.
_____	_____	I ask questions for clarification.
_____	_____	I show concern by acknowledging feelings.
_____	_____	I restate or paraphrase some of the speaker's words to show that I understand.
_____	_____	I seek first to understand, then to be understood.
_____	_____	I am poised and emotionally controlled.
_____	_____	I react nonverbally, with a smile, a nod, a frown, or a touch, if appropriate.
_____	_____	I pay close attention and do not let my mind wander.
_____	_____	I act responsibly with what I hear.
_____	_____	I don't change the subject without warning.

Bad Habits of Listening

On a scale of 1–5, with 5 being the worst, indicate the degree to which you are guilty of these poor listening habits. Rate yourself twice, first with the person you listen to the best and then with the person to whom you find it most difficult to listen.

Best   **Worst**

Best	Worst	
_____	_____	I interrupt often.
_____	_____	I jump to conclusions.
_____	_____	I finish other people's sentences.
_____	_____	I am parental and answer with advice.
_____	_____	I make up my mind before I have all the information.
_____	_____	I am a compulsive note taker.
_____	_____	I don't give any response.
_____	_____	I am impatient.
_____	_____	I lose my temper.
_____	_____	I think about my reply when the other person is speaking.

Some Helpful Listening Tips

- Be an active listener. Use good eye contact; nod your head; give some verbal cues that you are listening to the person.

- Show an interest in what the person is saying. Imagine yourself being faced with the same predicament.

- Listen to understand instead of listening to argue and judge.

- Don't let the other person's emotional display or choice of words throw you off course. Keep the purpose of the conversation clearly in the forefront of your mind. When necessary, keep the other person focused.

- Check out what you *think* you heard by restating what the other person said.

- Listen more intensely for *what* the person is saying instead of *how* he or she is saying it (for example, poorly enunciating, mispronouncing, or misusing words).

- When you need to gather more information, ask open-ended questions. (What? How? When? Why? Who?)

- When someone is angry, a good rule of thumb is to remain silent and listen to what he or she is saying—and, more important, what he or she is trying to say.

- Keep your emotions in check by taking an ongoing inventory of how you're reacting. Pay attention to signs like these:

  - Jaw muscles tighten

  - Stomach turns into knots

  - Breathing gets shorter and choppier

  - Hands get sweaty

  - Heart begins to pound

- At some point, your physical responses might be a clue that you are no longer actively listening to the person.

- When emotions get out of control, the purpose of the conversation typically gets lost. It might be best to end the discussion at that point and resume it at another time.

- Keep in mind that good listening is a skill and requires ongoing practice. So when someone comes into your office for a casual chat, make a point of giving this person your undivided attention—that means avoiding the tendency to want to continue typing, writing, reading, or filing papers while he or she is talking.

- When you give someone your attention, not only are you giving that person your time (a valuable premium), but you are also sending a complimentary message that you respect that person.

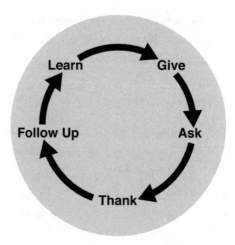

Figure A2-1 The Golden Circle of Strategic Networking

PART 3

Keep (Maintaining Your Hard-Earned Relationships)

10

Stay in Touch

*"The opposite of networking is **not** working—it takes time and effort that will pay off."*
—Andrea Nierenberg

T his section is probably the most compelling because you can spend a lot of time finding and growing your business through the relationships developed using the powerful art of networking. However, to see that everything is running productively, you must make sure that you keep your business and retain those amazing relationships and the business they've helped you develop.

It's time to explore creative ways to cultivate advocates in your networking relationships and be aware of continually identifying potential opportunities to do so. You'll find out how to earn referrals for your business and make sure everyone on your team realizes that they both help bring in business, as "rainmakers," and help to keep the business you have. You need to explore how to be proactive and stay in touch by remaining on your advocates', ambassadors', and clients' radar screens. You'll also learn how to manage all of this with your own contact management system—wherever you are conducting business.

Finally, you'll tie it all together and consider how to make networking part of your DNA (Dedicated Networking Always). You will learn my 10 easy-to-remember networking suggestions based on my acronym out of (what else?) the word *networking*.

Following up in a timely manner with materials promised, an immediate thank you note, or a "nice seeing you" note is a must for effective and strategic networking. The sure way to lose a contact is to fail to follow up and follow through. However, the next step is an equally important, yet often neglected action in today's busy world. This is the process of keeping in touch on a continual basis. Imagine how awkward it would be to contact someone you once met out of the blue and ask for a favor if you hadn't stayed in touch. This is an example of the kind of action that gives networking a bad name and makes people dislike these "What's in it for me?" types. Our surveys indicate that people are turned off by contacts who call or email them only when they need something. If you stay in touch with your networking contacts and nurture your network regularly, you'll receive a much more positive response to future requests.

Ways to Stay on Your Contacts' Radar Screen

To keep a relationship going, you need to stay connected. Recently a friend mentioned to me that although it's easy for her to send an email or a note after she meets someone, it's much harder for her to stay in touch after that. Follow-up, she told me, is reacting to a situation that calls for a response or action on her part. However, when she heard my comment about staying on your contacts' radar screen, she asked me, "After the follow-up, what 'opportunity' do I have to contact this person?"

"Sometimes," I told her, "you have to invent the opportunity, and you have to vary the contact methods."

If follow-up is reactive, think of staying in touch as proactive. It involves looking for ways to stay in touch and building on the relationship so that when an opportunity arises to ask for some advice, you can do it easily because you have a solid relationship. Here are some methods I use to stay connected.

Notes

Besides the thank you note, which is a follow-up must, you can send several other types of notes at any time to stay in touch, be helpful, and be remembered. Because handwritten notes are so rare, yours will really make an impression.

- **"FYI" (For your information).** Send articles to people in your network with a note saying, "I thought you might be interested in this." The articles can be related to the person's business or personal interests. I have a contact who is a huge Yankees fan, so I've sent him pictures from the Sunday newspaper and several articles on his favorite team. He's been appreciative of those, especially because I took the time to find out what he cares about. How did I remember what he likes? I wrote it all down, and now it's on my database under his name and information (look at the Client Profile Template in the Part 3 Appendix).

Other ways you can give your contacts helpful information is by sending them information from a seminar you've attended or forwarding information about an upcoming conference or class. Any information that helps them understand the latest trends in their business is good, too, and remember to send any helpful leads.

- **"Congratulations!"** Send a note of congratulations for a promotion, an award or honor, or an anniversary. I sent a former colleague a note of congratulations when I saw an article that a mutual contact, an editor we both knew, had written about him. I wrote to them both, congratulating my colleague on his promotion and complimenting my editor friend on his great article. It was a good opportunity to reconnect with both contacts and helped us keep in touch. My former colleague ended up hiring me for a project. He's a busy person, and although he might have considered me among others for his project, I clearly believe it was because we stayed in touch with each other. It made him think of me instead of my competition. He's also totally bottom line oriented—his emails are never more than about 10 words. I respond and write to him in exactly "his" way.

- **"Nice talking to (or meeting) you."** You can send these notes any time you speak with someone on the phone or at a meeting. I even send them after a chance encounter and conversation. I have some great note cards with a picture of a phone and "Nice talking to you" on the front. Use any technique you can think of to make you stand out from the crowd. I call this the power of "remember-ability." People are always amazed, and it reinforces our discussion and makes me stand out.

- **"Thinking of you."** I've found that when I send this type of note to people with whom I've not been in touch for a while, it often reopens the relationship. Laney had been a student in a presentation skills class years ago when she was in advertising. We stayed in touch at her next job, and then she started her own business—in, of all things, greeting cards. Now I'm one of her best clients.

- **"Wish you were here."** I send postcards wherever I go. I travel quite a bit and have found that this is a great way to stay in touch with contacts when I'm away from my office. My good friend and client Bob always sends me postcards from his world travels. He has a great system. He prints labels from his mailing list and takes them with him. Then he just writes the card and sticks a label on it. Easy!

You might be wondering how I have the time to send handwritten notes. I always carry notes and stamps with me. I use the time in airports, on trains, while waiting at the doctor's office, or while watching television to dash off a note, address it, and drop it in the mail. All it takes is carrying note cards in your networking toolkit, keeping a supply of stamps on hand, and, of course, being organized.

Holiday Cards and Special Occasions

Sending season's greetings cards to everyone in my network is a practice I have done for many years. I also send greeting cards on special occasions and other holidays. Many people throughout the world, for instance, celebrate Chinese New Year or the Jewish New Year (Rosh Hashanah), St. Patrick's Day, Mother's Day, or Veterans Day. I even send e-cards on Chocolate Day, if I know my clients like chocolate. (Yes, there is such a thing as Chocolate Day!) In fact, to be really creative, consult with Google or your favorite search engine—and type in "holidays" and see what comes up. There's usually a holiday daily.

Birthdays, anniversaries, and other important events are also opportunities to keep in touch with a note or small gift. Pay attention to what people mention about these dates. Some people are proud of work anniversaries, so you can send a note of congratulations on these occasions. Others mention an upcoming award, honor, or promotion. If you haven't heard about these important days from your contacts, you can find out about them from their coworkers, in articles, through Google Alerts, or from whatever the latest and greatest "search engine news aggregators" are. I've been collecting these days of importance for a while, and some months I send out as many as 80 personal greeting cards! My recipients continue to be surprised and happy to hear from me.

The key is to consider the profile and interests of your contact when sending a card. The card industry has millions of choices for you to give your contacts a little loving care—and to remind them of you.

BENEFITS OF SENDING GREETING CARDS

The Greeting Card Association tells us that sending a greeting card is a simple yet powerful gesture that reminds people someone is thinking of them. When you make someone else feel good, it also makes you feel good!

People often ask me how I find out my contacts' birthdays. I just casually ask them what month they were born after I've known them for a while. Then I record it in my client profile. My contacts usually forget they've told me their birthday.

Stay Connected

Set aside 10 minutes every day to reach out to a client, a prospect, and a new connection in their preferred method of communication to say hello and share an idea, thought, or suggestion. This is in addition to your regular calls and meetings for the day.

- Keep it brief and concise. You want to show they're on your mind.

- You can send an article, email, or quick message.

- Once a week, go through your universal list and call three people to say hello.

- Once every two weeks, have breakfast or lunch with a business friend, client, center of influence, or prospect.

Listen and Learn

We work on active listening skills, yet we sometimes forget to be totally involved in the process and exchange.

Track how well you're really listening with at least one call and interaction daily. Stop anything else other than writing notes as you listen. Focus on the message. If you're on the phone, note tone and inflection. If you're together in person, focus on the eyes to show you are connecting. (Hopefully you will do this with all interactions. Give yourself a daily goal, to be sure to monitor at least one—you'll see that it gets easier as you practice and focus.)

Learn at least one new piece of information daily as you connect. Write it down as you keep a running log of information learned. It can be a tip, an idea, a business strategy—the list is limitless. It's all in the focus and concentration.

Create Advocacy and Centers of Influence

Create advocacy and centers of influence as you build your brand and business. Think, "Who can I connect with each week?" Perhaps it's a center of influence with a client, a vendor or internal resource, or someone else. As you learn more about the people involved in your business, you will find opportunities to create other synergies and build your brand. Your advocates offer you valuable third-party endorsements and are part of your business marketing. Be their best ambassadors also—reach out to someone daily.

Do this monthly: List 10 contacts (clients, centers of influence, colleagues, friends). These are also your advocates. Ask these questions:

- How often are you two in contact?
- What is the biggest challenge the other person faces in business?
- When did you last visit the contact's website?
- What is one action item you can do for your contact in the near future:
  - Write an article.
  - Give him or her a referral.

- Help him or her solve a challenge.

- Have a face-to-face meeting.

Follow-Up

Follow up on something specific. Every day you follow up in your regular work, yet something on your desk right now needs a follow-up action. It could be from someone you met at an event, and this is your time to call or email. Maybe you have a connection that you promised to send an article or information. You might need to return a call or email, or link in. Whatever it is, besides everything you're doing in your action steps, you need to take five minutes to do one additional follow-up.

You have many creative ways to stay on your contacts' radar screen as you continually build and grow your relationships (you learn many things about your contacts) that will surprise and delight them when you pop up just to stay in touch and be on their radar.

- Set up a Google alert, to get an alert any time your contact appears in the media or anywhere on the Web. This gives you an opportunity to touch base—to say hello, offer congratulations, and so on.

- Adapt a list of topics to know about your connections over time. Create the ones that will be most important for you and an opportunity to be on the radar screen.

- Take time to reflect on what is important and of value in your life. I started my own "gratitude and nice card file," where I put a note each time I think of something for which I am grateful. Doing this is also a way to remember the strong personal connections I've created.

Reflect your own personality when reaching out to people.

Interesting Emails

Even though a handwritten note is a unique and thoughtful way to stay in touch, emails can also make you stand out. They can be used for the same reasons as notes, and you can use your own unique style to create them. Send links to interesting online articles and websites, inspirational quotes, pictures, and videos. You can also include articles, video clips, or pictures in the body of your email, with a personalized, friendly note on top.

Another way to use email to stay in touch is to let your clients know about any charity or community work you're doing. For instance, if your company is involved in a tutoring program, you can send an email to your clients about it, along with your note and pictures.

Many discussion forums and weblogs online cover a wide range of topics; find some that would interest your client. Start the email with something like, "I saw a discussion on this website about the distribution issues we were talking about. Thought you might be interested." Then include the link to the website.

I also use email to send monthly tips to people who have signed up for them on my website. Or you can include a signature at the bottom of your email that says, "Click here to get monthly tips." Some people send emails to their contacts every time their websites are updated with new information, products, or articles. Tweet and blog often to your network universe. Keep adding to your wealth of knowledge and expertise.

Whatever you do, make sure you have a valid reason for sending emails, and tailor your message to the recipient. Also remember to reply to emails within 24 hours of receiving them—even if only to acknowledge that you've received them—and promise to reply in detail later.

Your Own Article or Newsletter

If you've published an article in a trade publication or e-zine, email a copy of it to your contacts with a personal note. If you haven't yet gotten an article published, create your own. You can print it on nice stationery, email a copy to your contacts, or post it on your website and email your contacts the link. You can also post it on LinkedIn, Facebook, Twitter, and whatever the latest online vehicle is.

Gifts

Everyone enjoys a nice gift to celebrate a special occasion, such as the completion of a project, a promotion, a birthday or holiday, or someone doing a special favor for me. Sending a gift sets you apart, but you need to be careful about the nature of the gift. Keep in mind that this is a gesture of appreciation, and avoid placing the recipient in the awkward position of having to turn down your gift because of company policy. In general, food and flowers are good choices because the whole company can share them. I like to send a fruit basket, a tin of popcorn, a box of candy, or other goodies. I am also a big sender of the most delicious brownies. Of course, when your food gift is shared with others in the company, your name gets in front of others—an added bonus.

Make sure you consider the recipient's preferences and habits in deciding what gifts to send, and respect people's diets. These days, I'm careful to avoid giving candy or popcorn to clients who are watching their carbohydrate counts. I'm always on the lookout for items that people will like and can accept. One workshop participant told me about sending a bouquet of flowers to a client to thank him for some business. It turned out that his client was allergic to flowers. After the client's assistant assured him that a different plant was fine, he immediately sent one, along with an apologetic note. He then recorded his client's allergy in his client profile so he wouldn't make this mistake again.

I met one of my favorite vendors over the Internet when he emailed me to ask permission to use one of my articles in his newsletter. I was happy to do so and was in the market for a gift basket, so I tried it. (Pretty clever networking on his part!) Be creative with your food gifts. I've sent everything from chocolate telephones to fruit-flavored flowers.

Give the gift of a book that you like or one that has a special message. Send it with a note about why you thought your contact would also like it. People rarely throw away books; at the very least, they pass them along to someone else. I've actually incorporated what I call "give away a book a day to keep your networking growing day by day": Every week, I give or send a book as a gift to someone. I'm always reading and like to share with others.

I've given gift certificates so that people can choose what they want—all they have to do is order it. The fact that you ordered it at a store or website they like will show them that you went the extra mile. The important point is to do what works for you and makes your clients happy, and to keep it professional.

People in your network enjoy receiving gifts. Think of how the following words in this acronym can be a reminder when you are building your network.

GIVE A GIFT

G   **Giving gifts** that make you memorable

I   **Invite** and **involve** people in special events

F   **Friendly** people are giving people

T   **Time together** with somebody

Premiums

Invest in premiums with your company's name: pens, notepad holders, magnets, paperweights—anything useful and memorable. I give premiums to everyone who attends my seminars and to people I meet at events. Each premium has my name, company, and contact information, including my website. Most important, all my premiums are useful. My signature piece is a pocket mirror that says, "Can your smile be heard?" Every year I look for a new premium that will put my name in front of my contacts as they go about their working day. I love giving gifts that stay on people's desks. When they're functional, they're a constant reminder of your services.

Personalize each premium with a brief note and individualized message, just as you would for any gift.

Face Time

Despite the immediacy and efficiency of our online communication today, spending personal time with a client is memorable and more powerful. Finding the time to get together might seem difficult because we're all busy and live far apart. However, if you're persistent and creative, you can schedule these all-important personal meetings. Besides the traditional breakfast, lunch, and dinner meetings, suggest meeting for coffee or afternoon tea. Coffee shops are always in vogue for networking meetings. Or try playing a game of tennis or golf; going for a walk; meeting at a museum; getting a manicure; shopping; attending an industry event; or attending a play, concert, or sporting event. Share a cab to a meeting, or meet at the sky club at the airport when you're between flights in your colleague's city. Before going on a business trip or vacation, look up everyone you know in the places you'll be visiting; then call or email before going, to arrange meetings.

I had dinner recently in Atlanta with several business friends, found out they had common interests, and made a wonderful connection with each of them. Our telephones can now do all of this with ease through Facebook and LinkedIn. We can always be connected to our connections.

Everyone is busy, yet many still manage to spend time with people in their network. I meet with some people at least once a quarter and others a couple times a year. I see closer associates and friends more frequently.

Because of my travel schedule, I like to become familiar with, and then recognized at, the better restaurants and hotels for entertaining clients. I often find these through recommendations from people in my network. After eating or staying there, I send the hotel or restaurant manager a thank you note saying that I'll be visiting again in the near future. I have been happily surprised to receive very nice treatment when I return. Again, just showing appreciation and saying "Thank you" have set me apart and made these people remember me. It takes only a few minutes to do—and add their information to your Client Profile Template.

Here is a reminder of what to remember on every in-person connection. Enjoy it, be adaptable, connect and find community, and know when to go.

F.A.C.E. TIME

F   Make it Fun. Find unique things to do and places to meet.

A   Adapt to the other person's timetable and surroundings.

C   Connect and find common interests.

E   Know when to Exit—be respectful of the other person's time.

Share Your Expertise

I have a friend who is a consultant and a magician. He's often asked to perform his magic show at charity events, and he gives his time willingly. He contributes to the cause through his magic, stays in touch with people in his network, and even meets some new contacts at these events. He always walks away from these events with new business. People see him in action and remember him. What better way to build name recognition?

Think of your own expertise. When you offer your writing, proofreading, publicity, computer, or organizational skills, or any of your business or personal skills, you'll experience the satisfaction of knowing that you're helping others. When you take some time out of your hectic schedule to help someone else, you never know when the favor will be returned. Others appreciate and seek out knowledgeable people who want to give generously of their expertise. And when you've been a resource to people, they're more than willing to help you when you ask. Just avoid keeping score; do it because you want to help instead of keeping track of what is owed to you. Again, that says "negative networking" to me.

Technology

Videoconferencing, text messaging, and instant messaging are cost-effective and convenient. Whether you're using email, using the phone, or meeting face-to-face, decide what works best for you—and your contact—and what will make you stand out while maintaining meaningful personal contacts.

A DAILY, WEEKLY, AND MONTHLY PLAN TO STAY IN TOUCH

1. Every day, send an email to three people you haven't been in touch with for a while (or create variety with one note, one email, and one phone call).

2. Once a week, go through your contact list and reach out to three people just to say hello.

3. Once a month, have lunch with a friend, colleague, or client you haven't seen for a while.

4. Add or send a message to 10 people in LinkedIn or Facebook every month.

5. Write a quick how-to blog post or article for your own blog, e-zine, or fan page weekly.

6. Record a video tip about your own expertise, along with a call to action, and post it on YouTube, linking it to your social sites and blog.

Setting Up and Managing Your Contact Database

So many tools for managing your database effectively are right at your fingertips. I still keep my system simple, flexible, and usable for me. It's a part of my KISS theory (Keep It Simple, Sweetheart). My system for organizing and keeping track of a network database works on any system you have. I have a friend who says, "My life is in three different CRM programs in my office." It works for him, and he's very successful.

You can use any contact management application that works best for you. So many are available that I encourage you to consult with an expert or someone you trust to find out what might work best for you. The key for any type of contact management system is to find one method that's easy to use and that you can use consistently. The best networkers use a system that's organized and accessible.

I live with my iPhone for all mobile communication, and it has been my favorite tool. It took a long time for me to also give up my Blackberry, and now I can't imagine how or why I kept it for so long. More than 50% of our electronic communication is now done with a mobile device. That percentage is quickly growing, and so are the different versions and tools available.

Setting Up a Contact Database

Whatever formal system you decide to use, go back to the Client Profile Template and modify and insert it into your system to have all pertinent follow-up and "deepening the relationship" information that you need. I fill in as much information as I continually gather, and I also note whether they're introverts or extroverts so that I remember how to best communicate with them.

I continue adding information and meeting notes with the dates they occurred to the notes section. This gives me a complete record of interactions I've had with each person in my database. I also track how I came to know each person—who introduced us and how, when and where we met. This is critical information for my thank you chain contacts.

Prioritizing Your Network

My current database continues to grow, as I know yours will also. I'm frequently asked how I manage to keep in touch with all the people on my networking list. First, the majority of the people in my database comprise my mailing list, and I reach them regularly with my Tip of the Month.

I divide the rest of my list into three categories (A, B, and C), and I have a contact plan for each category. I organize all my contacts, professional and personal, in the same database because business opportunities can happen through different kinds of connections, and there's so much interchange and flow among various areas of my life.

My C list has people with whom I touch base. These are casual acquaintances with whom I am not currently doing business. They might also be former clients or people who are part of my thank you chain. I email each of them my Tip of the Month, and I send them a card or note once or twice a year, plus a holiday card. Currently, about 350 people are on this list.

My B list has "associates" with whom I am actively involved. I find a way to meet everyone on this list in person at least twice a year for a meal or coffee. I also send them at least six personal notes a year. If we're unable to get together, I call them every other month. I also send them holiday and premium gifts, my Tip of the Month, and a holiday card. This list includes about a hundred people.

My A list is made up of close friends and associates. I see each of them at least four times a year for a meal—or longer, if possible. I send them special gifts, holiday cards, and premiums, and I also frequently send them personal notes and articles. I look for opportunities to send flowers, theater tickets, or dinner certificates. I constantly think of ways to stay in touch with the 40 people on this list. They are my top ambassadors and advocates.

As you can see, because my contacts are categorized, I'm very realistic about how I can stay in touch with them in a quality way. I'm thrilled to have a huge contact base, yet the majority of these people are my electronic buddies—and the growing popularity of social media will only make this grow further. I'm often asked how many contacts I have on LinkedIn. I always say that, as with any network you build, it's quality versus just quantity. People have moved from this list to become closer associates when we've been in touch, they've followed up with me, or I've reconnected with them at an event or function.

These categories change continually because my network grows every day. I add new people to the appropriate category and move people between the lists, depending on what happens in life and how different connections occur.

My D list includes people who are no longer in my life, either for a period of time or forever. It's not personal. On the other hand, last year I reconnected with three people I knew from different venues 8, 10, and 12 years ago. They all reappeared at different times, and we just picked up where we left off. One of them has become a client, and I've been able to help another with a training plan for her company. I'm glad that all three are back in my life! That's one of the greatest parts of continual networking.

Birthdays

I keep track of birthdays by adding the contact's birthday month into the database. Then I create a birthday file in a simple MS Word file folder and make each month a separate document. Once a month, I print the list and mail each person a birthday card. Recently, I've started to add anniversaries and other special dates in the appropriate months, so I have all the important dates in front of me and can send my greetings. This makes it easy to remember. Plenty of software programs will do this for you, but my low-tech system still works for me.

Business Cards

The more you network, the more business cards you will collect, so you'll need a system to record all that information. Here's what I do when I get a card: I immediately add it to my database. Often I get a large stack of cards from people who simply want to be on the newsletter list. I go through these quickly, separate out the ones I made a connection with, and find an additional reason to follow up and say thank you. I send my follow-up notes and enter the information into my database, and I set the rest aside for my assistant to enter into the mailing database. With my iPhone, I also can add people immediately, and then it syncs with my Outlook system. Again, there are so many systems out today and another one tomorrow—find the one that works for you and develop it.

If the contact is going to become a client or prospect, I staple the card to a file folder in which I keep materials and other information. I put other cards into the "circular file" next to my desk because I've already captured the information in my database—and I like things to be clutter free!

Conversations and Meetings

I take notes on all the conversations I have, including business matters and important follow-up tasks and dates. I also enter any personal information, such as a favorite team, hobbies, or upcoming family celebrations. Again, refer back to the Client Profile Template that includes all these topics. These notes serve as conversation starters for the next time we meet, as well as reminders to send a note. I record all the notes in the Activities section of the contact's record in my computer database, including the date, purpose of the meeting, highlights of our discussions, and follow-up tasks and dates. I make sure I have a running log of every contact and conversation, and I always date them. Very often I also save our email correspondence in a folder, on my computer, with the person's name and company so that I have a complete information trail at my fingertips that's simple and organized.

STAYING IN TOUCH WITH A NEW CONTACT

When you meet someone at an event, do the following:

- Record the information from the business card in your contact database, or use one of the apps from your phone and sync to your database.

- Enter the date, where you met, and how (if it was through someone else), as well as notes about the person's profession, family, and interests.

- Record notes about your conversation.

- Send a "Nice to meet you" note.

- Mark down in your calendar that you will follow up in two weeks or when you both decide for a follow-up meeting.

On the Road

You live in a mobile world, and staying in touch with your universal network is easy, no matter where you are and in what time zone. Whether you take your laptop, your iPad, or just your phone, everywhere you go, there's an Internet connection. And that's all you need.

Between Go to My PC, Dropbox, and every other cloud connection, you can always be connected. This makes networking online so much easier and efficient.

Decide on the system that works for you and your organization. Being—and staying—connected is simple and also great for time management. Think when you're waiting in an airport or in your hotel room. Use all the different technologies and apps. Stay in touch, reconnect, start a conversation, go back to the Customer Profile template, and say hello to someone whose city you are visiting—and maybe set up a meeting.

The list is limitless—just start.

A Game Plan to Stay in Touch

Decide how often you want to contact the people in your universal network. I review my contact list every month. It usually takes a few hours, and I manage to do it by breaking it up into small blocks of time. First, I review every contact record to see if it's up-to-date, and I make any necessary category changes. Then I print or highlight the records for each of my A and B contacts. From this, I make a contact plan for the month. I determine whom I need to contact, why, and when, and I record on my calendar. My goal is to list at least nine people to contact every day during that month. It's what I call the Power of Nine.

As I add new people to my database, within 24 hours, I send them a "Nice to meet you" note or email to start the process. My calendar has follow-up dates and tasks that become a part of my daily "to do" list, the names of the nine people I should contact, and any cards I should send.

A TYPICAL DAY

Here's how I stay in touch on a typical day when I'm not in my office and at a client meeting:

- I check phone messages and prioritize them to determine who has to be called immediately.

- I return the priority calls right away and return the others within 24 hours.

- I check and respond to emails. For those that take more time, I send an email referring them back to later in the day.

- I call a prospect that has been referred to me. We speak briefly and set up a future phone appointment. This gives me a chance to check the prospect's website so I will be prepared when we speak. I also email the referral contact (his preferred method) to say thank you and ask if there is anything I need to know about the prospect. All this I record into my phone.

Then, when I return to my office, I make sure to do the following:

- Send the prospect a handwritten note.

- Send my referral source a handwritten note to thank him for the referral. I also utilize my automated software system, appreciationpower.com.

- Enter all the information into my database.

- Visit the prospect's website and prepare for our phone meeting the next day.

- Return the rest of my phone and email messages.

Staying in touch with everyone in your network is an art and a science. People like to be remembered and contacted in thoughtful ways. However, as your network grows, you need to create a system for staying connected with so many people. The successful networker knows how to combine these two tasks to create a seamless networking fabric in his or her life.

In the next chapter, you'll look at how to create your own "fan club," which involves building and maintaining a group of advocates who take it upon themselves to help you succeed in your business life. You also learn how to build your referral pipeline, develop a niche as you develop your network, and explore networking across the different generations.

Exercise 1: The Power of Three (or Nine)

The best way to stay in touch with people is to make a habit of contacting at least three of them a day by note, email, phone, or text. This enables you to make staying in touch a part of your busy schedule. Beside each category, write the name of at least one person to whom you will write a note, make a phone call, or send an email or text. You can extend this exercise by writing up to three people's names for each day of the week. Make a copy of this form, and do this exercise every day for a month, to make it a habit.

Coworker: _____

Prospect: _____

Client: _____

Friend: _____

Service Provider: _____

LinkedIn Connection _____

Contact from an Event _____

Family Member: _____

Note: I keep raising the bar for myself, and I have increased the Power of Three to the Power of Nine. Many of my colleagues and workshop participants have done the same. Take small steps—start with three a day, and make it a part of your life.

Inch by inch, it is a cinch—yard by yard, it is hard.

Exercise 2: Strengthening Your Network

The longer a working relationship has been in existence, the stronger it gets. However, it takes effort to make that happen. The following questions help you think about ways to build better and stronger connections with others.

What do you think are the three most effective ways to show appreciation after someone has given you business referrals?

_____

_____

_____

What are three important dates most people celebrate that you can recognize by sending a card, making a call, or sending a text?

_____

_____

_____

What could someone do for you that would justify sending a thank you gift? (List up to three.)

_____

_____

_____

11

Creating Advocates

"Create a mental picture with the word Success and stamp it indelibly on your forehead. Over time, you will begin to really see it."
—Anonymous

One afternoon, I received a phone call from the division of a large financial services firm asking me to come in for a meeting regarding an extensive consulting project.

During our conversation, I asked the representative how she had received my name and contact information. I knew that I could have cold-called and sent information and proposals for months and probably had no success. So why was I called?

I had an advocate at the firm: Erinn, a young woman I had helped several years ago after she attended a college class I was teaching on networking in business. Erinn was now a rising star at this firm, and she'd recommended me to her colleagues and to the selection committee.

I emailed Erinn immediately to thank her for the referral and said I would let her know what developed. As she later wrote back, "I never forgot how you helped me when I was starting out, meeting for a soda at the diner, listening, and offering your suggestions. You don't know how much I appreciated it."

Well, I do, and I'm thankful that Erinn is my advocate!

You know that networking is a necessary skill for finding and developing new clients and keeping those you have. It's also an opportunity to create advocates for your business. These advocates will be your best sales and marketing champions because they know and respect you.

They will talk about you and your business in a positive way. This is a credibility factor that no one can buy—it comes from working hard and smart to create powerful and strategic connections.

A colleague recently received an email with the subject line, "You come highly recommended." It was from the executive vice president of human resources for a large holding company, asking for a meeting to discuss her firm's products. As she read the email, she saw that a former client had referred her. As she said to me, "Even with both of our crazy schedules, we manage to keep in touch with each other in person or by email and notes." That client and I had met for breakfast not long before. After our breakfast meeting, he told a colleague about me, and I then received the email requesting a meeting.

Of course, even when you do have your advocates, you still need to market yourself directly to your prospects and clients. When your advocates open the door for you, you must stay in there and close the deal. It pays to create these advocates who believe in you and who can leverage your marketing efforts.

Identifying Potential Advocates

Creating advocates and ambassadors is key to expanding your networks. People who know you, trust you, and believe in you are all possible alliances and resources for you and your business. Look at the various people that are in your life.

The Satisfied Client

Who can be better advocates than satisfied clients or employers? They can give testimonials and refer you to others. Sometimes you might feel awkward about asking for referrals; however, there are ways to make asking easier. I had just finished a project at a new company where I had gotten to know several people quite well. While we were talking during our celebration lunch, I said, "As we debrief, tell me what you liked best about our program and what could have been changed or different." It was a positive discussion, and I thanked them all. Then I said, "I would be happy to work with anyone you feel comfortable referring me to within the firm." Two weeks later, I received a call from a colleague of one of the people at the luncheon asking me for an appointment to learn about my services.

Another time, I was referred to the former supervisor of a person I had worked with on a project. When Natalie called me, she said that Allison, who used to work for her, had recommended me to do the same project for her organization. Of course, I thanked both Natalie and Allison, and I kept Allison in the loop as the project progressed. Your advocates stay with you when you stay in touch. This is part of the thank you chain we talked about in Chapter 9, "Follow-up: A Road Map for Growth." Be sure to always keep everyone in the loop and in their preferred communication method.

Good times to ask satisfied clients for referrals are after a success, when you're meeting during a social gathering, and when you've solved any challenges that might have occurred.

People You Work With: Your Team

Whatever someone's job description might be, it's ultimately a sales job. You might be thinking, "Wait—my assistant doesn't sell" or even "I don't sell." What does sales have to do with that type of job? Anyone who has a client contact, whether direct, as in sales and customer service, or indirect, as in production or accounting, is ultimately responsible for selling and marketing the company. In fact, as you build your internal networks and alliances, you are always selling ideas to others, so you are in sales. You need to help everyone around you think like this. Your assistant might speak all day to your clients, internal support teams, and management. The way he or she communicates is a direct reflection of you. Empower your team members to think of ways to create and develop more business opportunities, regardless of their job function.

Conrad Hilton built his hotel empire on the principle that every employee is responsible for sales, from the groundskeepers, housekeepers, and bellhops, to the front-desk staff. Every interaction with a customer is a sales opportunity, even if that is well-kept ground, spotless rooms, or a smile and greeting at each contact.

If everyone on your team could think, "How is what I'm doing helping the client, whether internal or external?" then everyone would be an advocate for your firm. Helping an internal client—coworkers who depend on you to help them get their jobs done—is as important as helping an external client. First and foremost, you must build and maintain a strong foundation.

Creating advocates in your company takes the same networking skills we've been discussing. Find out who you need in your network, and get to know them—listen and learn. Then make the connection and stay in touch. Go through the same processes we've been discussing. Think of every meeting as an opportunity to further build your internal network.

EVERYONE IS IMPORTANT

Too often people network only up the corporate ladder. My theory is that every single person is important and is part of your internal team. Smart people know to build relationships and alliances with those up, down, sideways, and across. Create and build relationships throughout the company.

Contacts and Colleagues in Your Business or Industry

In today's world, many of the contacts you make in your industry will refer business to you because you specialize in an area that is needed. Here's where your self-marketing skills are necessary. Fine-tune your 30-second infomercial, become known in your field by giving presentations and writing articles, join and participate in professional organizations, and follow up and stay in touch with your network contacts.

Judy, a woman I met in a yoga class, had launched a photography business. Several years later, she now has a successful portrait studio. Much of her business comes from referrals from other photographers who specialize in commercial work. They refer their clients to her for portraits and executive head shots, and she refers clients to them for websites and corporate photography. She's a specialist in her area and has a reputation as one of the best. The key here is to identify what you do best and to make sure that becomes your "brand"—when people need what you do, you will pop up on their radar screen.

Others at Your Client's Place of Business

It's important to reach beyond your comfort zones and meet more people, develop more relationships, and learn that, even with your strongest business accounts, it's critical to "surround the account" and know several people at the firm or organization. Think of the different people at a firm you meet during a job interview, or those you're working with on a specific account, or the different people on the internal team. Get to know the different people as you build your networks.

At one firm I work with, Linda used to be my main contact, Claudette was her assistant, Alice worked next to her, and David and Michael were assistants. By creating and developing relationships with all these people and staying on their radar screens, I have expanded my network and set the scene for more business. Recently, Linda left the company and went to another one. I kept in touch with her and will soon be presenting a proposal to her new company. Claudette, her assistant, was promoted, and because of my relationship with her and others, I have kept my business at that company. This is a story that has been around for ages. Every person who takes on a leadership role brings in his or her own teams. Make sure you've done your homework to know them.

Several years ago, I helped Carol find a new job. Then she introduced me to the head of marketing in her company, who hired me to do a program on presentation skills. In the last few years, I have done many projects with this company. Carol left the firm after a year, yet because I created many internal connections in the company, I have worked in all its branches throughout the country. I continued to work with Carol in her next job, which was more suited for her. Now she's thinking of starting her own business in the next year, and she knows that I will be one of her biggest advocates, as she has been for me.

START YOUR THANK YOU CHAIN

1. Think right now of all the connections you have within a firm.

2. Go back and put into action the thank you chain to touch base with some of these people. Connect to say thank you—call, write, text, email, or use social media. Just do it!

3. Then before you do anything else, go back to your contact management system and enter the names of these people, your relationship to them, how you know them, and what business you might have gotten from or given them. (Use the Client Profile Template in the Part 3 Appendix.)

4. Watch the relationships in each of your accounts begin to multiply, and see your network grow.

How many times have you lost business when your main contact left the company? You have to start all over again to win back the account. Better to have advocates throughout the organization who will champion your services.

Think of the companies you work for now and possible advocates you have developed. Remember to use your thank you chain, and be sure to show your appreciation for referrals others give you. Keep this information in your contact management system, and stay in touch. Business can come from anyone on the other side of your door.

Your Friends and Neighbors

You work hard at building friendships that include mutual trust and respect. As you find out more about your friends' work, you'll want to help them, and over time, they will most likely want to help you with referrals.

Recently, my friend Norma experienced some challenging times in her business. She lost several key clients through circumstances that had nothing to do with her ability. I introduced Norma to another friend of mine who was looking for a top person in his company. Now Norma is working there happily, and she has also become my advocate. I spoke at a meeting of one of her industry organizations, which resulted in three new contacts for me. We both make sure we stay on each other's radar at all times.

Turning neighbors into advocates might take more time, yet it will be worth the effort. Take the time to strike up conversations with people in your building or neighborhood. Often you find that you have common interests.

My friend Jan struck up a conversation with a young man in her elevator and found out that he was a coin collector. She knew someone else whose hobby was coin collecting and arranged to have the young man attend a showing. His parents were so impressed with Jan's gesture that they invited her and her husband for cocktails at their home. During the evening, they discovered they shared a lot of common interests. The young man's father is the managing partner at a large law firm, and Jan is a publicist who works with law firms. Several months later, Jan has this firm as a client, along with another firm the father referred to her. Like Jan, when you look at life with a networking awareness, your contacts will develop into something more.

You never know what can happen when you get to know your neighbors. It all starts with a smile, genuine interest and curiosity about others, and self-marketing skills to create advocates. We meet people in a variety of ways, develop relationships, and then see opportunities present themselves—often when we least expect it.

People many times ask me the underlying question, "How do I convert a friendship into business without jeopardizing the friendship?" We never want our friends to think we are exploiting our relationship, and we also may worry that a poor result will sour the friendship. The remedy for this dilemma is twofold. Half is mindset, and half involves tactics.

Think about the following:

- Your friend might have a need for what you or your firm specializes in. You already have a vested interest in your friends, and you can say that you would like to refer them to a trusted source that you work with.

- Your friend might also wonder why you haven't brought up the subject in the past.

- You are successful at what you do and consider that working together might actually deepen your friendship because your friend will see you in a role in which you shine.

When you develop a different mindset, you are ready to plan a strategy for suggesting that you work together. Preplan the conversation in your mind, to make you more comfortable in something that you might perceive to be an awkward discussion.

Here's one approach:

> Elizabeth, I'd like to talk about the possibility of our doing business together, and I don't want it to impinge on our friendship. Would it be okay to come to your office on Tuesday and discuss your financial/estate planning needs to see if there's an area in which my firm or I might be able to help you?

This approach has several advantages:

1. It clearly acknowledges that you value the friendship and don't want to jeopardize it.

2. It lets your friend know that you recognize the boundaries between friendship and business, and it makes clear that you do not intend to convert your "friend time" into an endless barrage of sales pitches.

3. It puts you on a businessperson-to-businessperson footing when talking business.

If even that approach seems too direct, here are some other ways to get friends to start thinking of you as the solution to their business concerns instead of seeing you as just a great tennis partner or another mom on the soccer sidelines:

1. Ask them about their businesses. This typically leads to questions from them about your business.

2. The next time you're scheduled to have lunch, ask them to meet you at your office. When they see you in your business environment, they might see you in a new light.

3. Showcase your business acumen by inviting them to a seminar put on by your firm at which you are a featured speaker.

4. Forward an article of professional interest to them that relates your expertise. Include a personal note highlighting why it might be of interest to them and how it relates to your practice.

5. Invite them to be your guests at a business-related program on a topic of mutual interest. Picking up the tab sends the subtle message that you consider this a business opportunity.

Which friend have you overlooked as a great prospect for your services? What could you do this week to broach the possibility of doing business together? With the right mindset and approach, doing business with friends can be comfortable, fun, and profitable!

Building Your Referral Pipeline

Positive networking is your way of marketing yourself. You build business when you receive referrals from your clients, contacts, and friends. They believe in you so much that they want to send opportunities your way.

Sometimes they need a reminder—and that's why it's so important to stay on people's radar screens: You want to come to mind when they want someone with your expertise. When others take the time to refer you, it means they trust you because you have earned that trust.

Here are some ways to earn trust and stay on your contacts' radar screens every day:

1. Get to know your clients as friends. Have a meal with them, take them to an event, and develop a relationship with them as you would with a friend.

2. Provide service that dazzles your clients. Credibility is everything. Make it easy for them to brag about you because you provide top service and always go the extra mile.

3. Always think of them and what they need. Be proactive. Think of how you can make their life and work easier and more productive. Be the go-to person to fix things for them.

4. Continually give added value. Whatever you currently do for them, do some more and spice it up. Send them a note or a tip of the month (or week) to keep them informed about things they want to know and information that could help their business.

5. Make connections for them. Help them find new business, a valuable connection, or anything that enhances their life or solves a problem.

6. Never keep score. Do it because you like and respect them. If you show that they're always on your radar screen, you will find yourself on theirs as well.

Over time, you will earn their trust and respect and will see the results in a solid network of contacts that you can rely on and go to when you need help. From time to time, however, you might want to ask your clients and contacts for a "report card." Find an appropriate time to ask the following questions:

- What makes you do business with me?

- What could I be doing better?

- When you refer me to someone, what qualities about me come to mind?

Always remember that a referral is earned and is never given without thought and consideration. Here's a checklist of more suggestions on how you can grow your referral pipeline without asking for them:

- Make a daily thought of "Who will I meet today?" or "Who will I be introduced to today?" At the day's end, have a friend or family member ask you, "Who were you introduced to today?" This just helps keep your awareness and focus more in tune.

- Fall in love with the word *curiosity*. It's a great probing word, and people are more likely to open up when we're curious. It also works well with any objection. "I see. Tell me more—I'm just curious."

- Make sure your advocates and ambassadors know how to refer you and know that you are a reflection of their trust when they do refer you.

- Keep them in the loop. I know I say this a lot, but it is important.

- Receive every referral graciously. How you receive the referrals you get will either encourage or discourage your contact, client, or networking resource for future referrals.

- When the referral turns out favorably, offer to take both your source and the new contact to lunch. This makes it more collaborative.

- Become proactive at giving first. Always ask others, 'How do I know when I'm speaking with someone you would like to meet?" and "How do I know your ideal client or someone who can use your services?" Give first and build on the relationships, and the referrals will come. Even if you can't always give other people a concrete referral, you're letting them know that they're on your radar and that you want to know how to introduce them when the opportunity arises. One of my dad's greatest lines has served so well in receiving referrals: "Give without remembering, receive without forgetting."

- Strive for introductions with your strongest clients and advocates. In conversations, you might ask, "What made Bill come to mind? How do you know him, and what will make him take my call?"

Networking Across Generations

You currently interact with four generations, especially at work: Millennials, Generation X'ers, Baby Boomers, and Traditionalists. Whatever generation you are in, you look to the others as different and have to adjust.

Phyllis Weiss Haserot, Practice Development Counsel Consulting/ Coach to the Next Generation, says that networking and dealing with people of different generations is similar to the recipe for any kind of successful networking—with a few twists. Have a sincere interest in the other person. If you really want to learn about their interests, how you can help them, what makes them tick, it will show. (If you're bored and uncomfortable, that will show, too.) Ask questions about them with enthusiasm.

Here's what Generations X and Y and Millennials want:

- To feel important
- To be heard
- To have their ideas sought out
- To feel respected and valued

- To feel that you enjoyed the conversation

- To sense your authenticity

When you're networking, if you know people in the room, introduce the young people to them. Make those people feel comfortable by telling a snippet about them, to lay a foundation for common ground or a conversation starter.

Also offer to introduce your new young acquaintances to people outside the event. They're hungry to build their networks and learn from experienced people, and your offer shows that you respect them and the value they might bring to an older person. Don't worry about having to be an expert in their music, sports, or other interests if you don't really care to be. That's inauthentic, and they will pick up on it.

One of the keys is to get outside yourself and feel excited by what you can learn about and from each new person you meet. It's a state of mind that you can adopt if it doesn't come naturally. I'm lucky that it does come naturally to me. I feel fortunate to have many good friends who are much younger than I am, and I love their company and hanging out with their friends. We energize each other, and it's a great feeling.

Creating Rainmakers in Your Business

A rainmaker is someone who thinks about growing the business and finds ways to bring it in continually—someone who generates opportunities for new and current clients and thinks of ways to solve their problems. If everyone on your team did this, business would improve. To help everyone think like a business developer, you need to create awareness and communicate the idea to your team.

An accounting department manager at one company I know trains her team to speak in "user-friendly" terms to customers. Instead of calling only to ask about payment, her team listens to the clients to understand their problems and finds ways to solve them. The team members have come to see how everything they do, from the way they speak to clients, to the way they handle complaints, has a direct connection to the bottom line. While listening to a client's questions about a transaction, one staff member discovered both a concern and an opportunity for new business. She handled the concern and relayed the conversation to staff members who were able to correct a problem that could have lost the business. They were then able to take advantage of an opportunity that created new business. This staff member in accounting now truly believes and understands that she is part of the rainmaking team and understands the value of internal networking.

> The dictionary definition of *rainmaker* is "a person (as in a law firm) who brings in new business; also: a person whose influence can initiate progress or ensure success."

Salespeople work hard to sell and create relationships with clients, yet everyone in the company also needs to build and maintain good relationships with clients. Everyone is in sales. The operations manager, the marketing associate, and the IT technician represent the company every time they contact a client or a potential client. I like to say that we are all in sales, public relations, and customer service for the companies with which we work. In fact, customer service isn't a department—it's part of everyone's job, from the CEO down to the receptionist.

A dentist I know embraced the concept of rainmaking when she was losing patients because of the way her office staff treated them. In one case, a patient who left also took five family members, three people from her office, and two friends from her health club! My friend was fortunate to find out about this, since most people who receive poor treatment don't complain; they simply go away and then tell everyone about their experience. The dentist took immediate steps with her staff to correct the way they were handling patients and to stress the importance of their role in the practice. She was able to turn them into rainmakers.

People on your team need to know and understand a couple ideas to think like business developers and strategic networkers. And if your "team" is only you, then you'll have to work even harder and smarter because you are your business and you are the product. First, ask what business you're in, whom you serve, what your clients' needs are, who your competitors are, what makes you different, and what unique benefits clients derive from your services. Second, ask what your mission statement is and how that applies to your clients.

At one company I recently worked with, I asked the group to tell me its mission statement; only 2 out of 40 people knew it, and most had no idea how it applied to them. It's your job to explain your mission and turn your employees into advocates. Look at your employee roster. How well do you know the employees who are in a position to relay your message? What can you do to incorporate some networking techniques into your day by going to a different area and spending a little time with each employee or department? I read that Sam Walton, the late founder and CEO of Walmart, not only knew the name of each of his employees, but also empowered them with a sense of ownership of their company. To this day, when I walk into a Walmart, I always feel welcome, as if each person contributes to all the great customer service and sales there. I'm glad I also own stock in the company!

Find ways to listen to your team and hear their concerns and problems. It's important that you know how they interact with customers and that they understand how their relationship with customers affects the company. When people feel their work is important, they become advocates for the company, which is the ultimate in building relationships.

Give members of your team some appreciation; find ways to say thank you and to compliment them. Be sure to compliment them when they handle clients well or when they're advocates for your business. Studies show that people often work harder when they feel appreciated and that behavior that is rewarded is repeated. Instill in your people the power of networking and that it is everyone's job. Reward them when they succeed at it. Lead by example.

SEVEN STEPS TO CLIENT RETENTION

1. Spend 20 minutes daily talking with two existing clients or networking connections. Ask them what they want, what they need, what they like, and what they dislike. Ask them how they feel about the service they're currently receiving. Listen, implement changes, and suggest new ideas.

2. Invite your "champion clients" to serve on an advisory board.

3. Partner with your client in a workshop or special event. The more time you spend together, the more you bond.

4. Provide value every day. Offer something unique to show that you are creative, resourceful, and open to new ideas.

5. Find ways to connect on common ground, such as through hobbies, sports, special interests, religious affiliations, or school alumni groups.

6. Spend some time with your competitors and learn what they're doing. Find out from your clients what they hear in the outside world.

7. Conduct regular client satisfaction surveys or interviews, both formal and informal. These also provide valuable feedback.

Grow and Keep the Business You Have

Getting new business is much tougher than growing, managing, and building the business you already have. What can your team do to grow existing business?

1. Make your relationship with your customer's job number one. Find ways to stay focused on the client. I know one firm that only calls or emails clients at billing time. Needless to say, several clients have found other firms—ones that they feel are there for them in between the billing periods.

2. What do your clients need? What worries them? When you provide solutions, or at least show them that you care, you become a valuable addition to their team.

3. Who are your best customers, and why do they buy from you?

The principal objective of developing customers is to focus on the customers' needs. Happy customers are then cultivated as tremendous referral sources. When you have a customer on your side, generating high-profit word-of-mouth referrals is always easier. At the same time, your employees can be thinking beyond current ideas about what to do and how to help when they hear clients' concerns, problems, or situations (positive or negative). This affects everyone's job by contributing to the bottom line.

We all want personal attention, and we are all someone's customer. See how you feel the next time someone you work with treats you well or not so well. You might consider assigning every customer someone whom they can call at any time, so at least there's always a "real person" to help. If that person is unable to handle the situation, he or she can direct the call to someone who can.

Your personal advocates can offer you the most valuable third-party endorsements. Think of them as part of your personal "buzz marketing" campaign. Be sure to take good care of the connections you have with them.

It's hard to believe that it's time to wrap up everything we've discussed so that you can build on what you've discovered to create a terrific networking future.

Exercise: Who Are Your Advocates?

1. List 10 contacts (clients, coworkers, employees, friends) who are advocates for you and your business. What quality made you think of them?

2. How often are you in contact with each of them?

3. What is the biggest challenge each of them faces?

4. What associations or organizations do they belong to, and have you been to a meeting? Recently?

5. When did you last visit their website or respond to something you saw on Google Alerts?

6. List at least one thing you could offer to do for them in the near future:

   a. Write an article for a publication.

   b. Offer to do a workshop pro bono.

   c. Send an article of interest.

   d. Give them a referral.

   e. Make a useful introduction.

   f. Help them solve a problem.

   g. Send a card or note for a special occasion.

"When all is said and done, much more is said than done."
—Anonymous

12

Today, Tomorrow, and Your Future

Each day holds amazing networking opportunities for you. It truly is a small world, and you never know what will come from the connections or contacts you make. This is part of the fun of life, and I always hold on to that wonderful phrase, "If you want to make God laugh, tell him your plans." We just never know what's in store for us and how our lives can change or be enhanced, or how something entirely new can suddenly unfold. This can happen just because someone we've met makes a connection for us, we've reconnected with an old friend, or we've met someone through a chance encounter. Of course, much of this has to do with our following up. Things happen when we take that action step after life has presented us with a variety of opportunities.

In business, which is such an integral part of our lives, the power of connection is the key. It's all about whom you know, and who knows you, and how you enhance and learn from those relationships. Often in my workshops, I ask, "Is it always the smartest person who rises to the top of an organization?" Unanimously, people say, "No!" The truth is that being smart and capable is your ticket in the door and staying there. However, to succeed and keep building your business, you also need to have great alliance and people skills—just what we've talked about throughout this book. The philosophy is simple; it's the consistent implementation that takes discipline.

In today's crazy, time-starved world, people want information quickly and succinctly so they can act on it. Did you know that Abraham Lincoln's Gettysburg Address was a total of 226 words, and the Ten Commandments only 297 words? These are documents that get their points across succinctly.

EVERYONE HAS A MOTHER...

Having just reconnected with a friend about a year ago, I established a business relationship with the association she heads. I met her second-in-command, Marshall, who, when not working for the association, runs his own marketing company. Just recently, Marshall hired me to conduct a media training program for one of his clients, a doctor.

As it turns out, I told the doctor during our session that his last name was uncommon and that I also knew a very nice woman with the same last name in the direct marketing industry, where I started my career. I asked him if he knew her. "Yes," he said, "she's my mother!" Life is funny. You never know when one connection may lead you to another.

Another time, sitting in a client's office, I was looking at his family picture and saw his sister. This was another great experience. I knew her from an industry association where I had been active. However, she has a different last name, lives in another city, and works in a different industry. I just was being observant and commented on the picture. What are the odds that I would have been in her brother's office?

Again, you just never know. The world is truly connected.

WHEN YOU NEED A RELATIONSHIP, IT'S TOO LATE TO BUILD IT

Live life with the state of mind that networking is everything—it is life. Greet each day with a "networking eye and ear." Learn and be aware. To do this, incorporate these practices daily—or at least be aware of them:

1. Meet people and nurture your current network.

2. Listen to and learn from all the people you connect with.

3. Make connections for others.

4. Follow up.

5. Stay in touch.

New stories and "aha" moments happen every day. People like you connect with me all the time to tell me of their success. Often they realize that they have been networking all along and never realized it, or they tell me how they have become more aware of this interesting phenomenon and state of mind. I especially enjoy when they tell me about their best practices and success stories, and how they've passed them down to their staffs, colleagues, and teams at work.

You've been on quite a journey in this book. Very simply stated, you have gone through tips, strategies, and techniques for finding, growing, and keeping your business through the art and science of networking. The magic formula for all this is in the doing of it. Start today with your awareness of it all, and just remember these final few facts.

Networking is truly a misunderstood word. Yes, some work is involved, and when you implement what we've discussed in this book, you will see results over time and without keeping score. Just try to be aware of everything and live life with your networking eyes and ears open. Continually do your homework—always be prepared and organized, and consistently apply the techniques we've discussed in your daily life.

Whenever I give a speech or a workshop, I always finish my program with what I call my Networking Acronym. It really condenses everything we've discussed in this book to its simplest form, and I hope you can take one thought, one idea, or one "aha" moment from it and put it into action starting today. And if you come up with some thoughts that I've left out, please connect with me and let me know, and I will add them into my next speech, workshop, or seminar.

N   Remember people's **names**. To each person, his or her name is golden. On that same thought, continually **nurture** the relationships of your current networks and find out what they need.

E   **Enthusiasm** and **energy** are key; have the **empathy** to understand that everyone has his or her own agenda; remember that **eye** contact speaks volumes; and know when to **exit** gracefully. **Execute** the skills, **engage** in the process, and realize that it **evolves** over time.

T **Talk** less and listen more. Networking is about listening and learning from everyone you meet. Developing **trust** takes **time**, and you always need to be in the mode of **thinking**, "How can I help this person?"

W **Write.** In this electronic age, a handwritten note or message stands out and will be remembered. **Work** is involved that you will incorporate into your daily life.

O **Organization** is key. Keeping your contacts, records, and information is essential to your success. Remember, whenever you meet others, it is an **opportunity** to learn from them and be a resource to help them. To do this, get into the habit of asking **open-ended**, high-gain questions to develop rapport.

R **Research** everything. Know that the goal is to develop a **rapport** that will lead to a **relationship** encompassing both trust and **respect**. Your **reputation** is crucial because you have built on it your whole life, so be careful when you **refer** anyone—that person is a **reflection** on you. Be **resilient** and **respectful** of all. Everyone has a lesson to teach us.

K **Knowledge** is power...only with execution. Much of our discussion has been common sense—it's just not always common practice. Take the action steps to make things happen. Keep in touch, and be creative about it. Also, I think every day about what my wonderful father said to me and continues to say as he smiles down from heaven: Be kind to people; give everyone you meet a smile and a handshake. My dad was the master of this and lives in my heart daily.

I **Integrity** is everything we have discussed. Your character and reputation are so important—remember that, with integrity, nothing else matters. To make your networking work, be sure to always take the **initiative**. Waiting for someone else to make the first move is not the style of a proactive networker. Also, become **interested** in other people and what you can learn from them.

N Sometimes you have to say **no**—when you say yes to everyone, you say no to yourself; know your limits. On the other hand, when I hear "No," I often reverse the letters to *on* so that I am resourceful and creative in making and keeping my connections.

G Set **goals** for your networking achievements, and remember to show **gratitude** to those who help you. Also **give** of your time and expertise to others. In the end, it's all about **going** for it and being **gracious**.

One Final Story: How Networking Has Changed My Life

I remember March 1993 very well. I had been working as a magazine publisher and was enjoying my work very much. Then one day that March, I received a phone call. It caused me to remember a promise I'd made to myself a few years earlier after I was in a bad car accident and had to be hospitalized.

I'd promised myself that I'd start my own business. I didn't know how, but I did know that this was what I really wanted to do in life. In fact, I had been preparing myself all along as a student of psychology and business. I had already been speaking publicly through my work at a variety of associations and at any opportunities that popped up. I had also started teaching other workshops, yet I had not taken that leap of faith.

When that call came, it was from one of my publishing clients, Max, who was asking me to come and speak to his sales staff at their annual meeting. That morning, as I was reviewing my notes for my presentation, I had a funny feeling that this experience might change my life. Fast-forward to the next day. The presentation went very well, I thought.

Apparently, Max did as well. Afterward, he invited me in as a consultant and said, "We will be your first client." And for three years, two days, and a week, his company helped me lay the groundwork for my business. This gave me the opportunity to interact with a whole company of people—from the junior people who were just starting out and learning some of the rules of business etiquette, to the senior people who needed

---

to brush up on their presentation and pitching skills and wanted to learn how to work more effectively with their growing staffs.

As I met and worked with each person, I learned so much about each of them and practiced all the techniques and strategies outlined in this book. The 200 or so people with whom I worked there started another huge network in my life and business. People I had connected with left and went to other companies and brought me in to work with them and their teams (hence the beginning of my thank you chain).

During the three years I worked at that company, I also worked diligently on figuring out what other industries I most wanted to work in. I practiced my 2-2-2 strategies, went to a lot of meetings and associations, met a lot of people, and then decided to join several organizations and become involved. More doors opened, and the very steps we talked about in Part I, "Find (Meeting People)," became, and still are, a devout daily practice of mine. I realized there was, and is, so much opportunity everywhere when you just take the time to live life with a networking eye and ear as I have learned to do—by offering to give first and be a resource to others.

After my accident, while I was lying in the emergency room of a local hospital, in Massachusetts, waiting to be airlifted to one of Boston's top hospitals, I asked the doctors to call my parents so they would know what was happening. I still remember what my father, who had been recuperating from open-heart surgery, said to me as they held the phone to my ear: "Keep fighting—you are my whole life."

Through the years, I have thought about what my dad said and how I promised myself that when I got well, I would go out, find a way to make a real difference, and give back to all the people who have helped me along the way. For me, being able to give back like this has been one of the most fulfilling parts of being alive. I now realize how this attitude and my dad's loving words really are what changed my life and made me want to be a giver as much as I possibly can. To me, that is what networking is really all about. The human relations principles we discussed in this book are all practices we can use in our lives every day. You will see, or you have already seen, how everything we do is linked to others in our life—the way we touch them or the way they touch us—and how we influence them and they influence us.

As I look at my business and how it continues to grow, I see that every single aspect of my life relates to finding, growing, and keeping lasting, powerful relationships. These have opened doors for me and created amazing opportunities. My hope is that you will close this book now and promise to act on some of the tips, ideas, and strategies we have discussed and then contact me and let me know about all the wonderful successes that continue to come into your life.

Thank you for the opportunity to come into your life through this book, to share and discuss some of the interesting business strategies and lessons I have learned along the way from the many masters who have touched my life.

Exercise 1: What Do You Think Now?

Now that you've finished reading this book and doing the exercises, think about how your thoughts on networking might have changed. Please answer the following questions:

How has your definition of networking changed? How can you now create more business opportunities and stronger personal relationships through your own power of networking? What are you going to do consistently?

_____

_____

_____

List three new ideas about networking that you've learned.

1. _____

2. _____

3. _____

Exercise 2: Know Yourself

When you know effective networking techniques, you can use them in any situation. Wherever you network in business and in life, remember the following:

1. **Know who you are.** Write down, in one or a few lines, how you want people to remember you. What would people say were your positive personality attributes?

_____

_____

_____

2. **Focus on others.** Write down your best conversation starters.

_____

_____

_____

3. **Have a goal.** Which goals are you most concerned with now in your life?

   a. Promotion

   b. New job

   c. Political aspirations

   d. Career change

   e. Lifestyle change

   f. New business venture

   g. Move to a new location for work and/or life

   h. Clients for your business

   What can you do today to start achieving those goals?

_____

_____

_____

Exercise 3: Do It Today

Which person will you contact today whom you haven't thought of before you did these exercises? Write down that person's name, how you will contact him or her, and what you want to accomplish.

_____

_____

_____

_____

The Networking Acronym: Fill in any other traits or techniques that come to mind. Take the next step, and write next to each letter an experience that corresponds to that letter, to make it real for you.

For example...*E*: Remember a time when you had a successful *exit* strategy. Or *W*: Think where you started the process of *writing* handwritten notes. Keep this going for yourself to maintain a networking tip log.

N _____

E _____

T _____

W _____

O _____

R _____

K _____

I _____

N _____

G _____

Exercise 4: Networking Action Plan

As a result of reading and working through this book, what are you going to do in the *first week*?

More of:

_____

_____

Less of:

_____

_____

Change:

_____

_____

By the *end of the month*, I will:

Do more of:

_____

_____

Do less of:

_____

_____

Change:

_____

_____

In the *next three months*, I will:

Do more of:

_____

_____

Do less of:

_____

_____

Change:

_____

_____

Remember, positive networking is all about giving more to others than you receive and always being a resource for them. Until we meet again, all the best in your networking!

Appendix

Client Profile Template

As you build your network connections and turn them into relationships, the more you know about someone the better. Collect data through conversations over time, and then you can use it to reach out, show that you remember important information, and continue to build the relationship.

Business Information

- Company/firm

- Business background and previous work experience

- Address and phone number

- Assistant's name

- Promotions and business opportunities

- Key relationships

- Corporate culture, levels, and politics

- "Why do you work with us?"

- How you met

- Business issues they are working on now

- Who you refer them to and why

- Immediate business and career objectives

- Personality type: Driver, Expressive, Analytical, Amiable

- Did you ask for their advice? Information given?
- How you've handled challenges in the past
- Which competitor they're most concerned about
- How they receive information: online, print, TV/radio
- What contributions are they most proud of?
- Preferred method of communication: email/phone/text/other
- Anniversary of doing business together
- What motivates them
- What achievement makes them proud
- Professional associations

Personal Information

- Birthday
- Birth state or country
- Activities in the community and charities
- Education: high school, college, fraternity or sorority, degrees
- Military service
- Hobbies and personal interests
- Favorite foods and restaurants
- Vacation interests
- Spouse: name, occupation, and interests
- Children: ages, names, schools, and interests
- Pets
- Personal objectives
- Key extended family members
- Special holidays
- Any specific likes and dislikes

- Book genre that they enjoy reading

- Collections they have

- How often they want to be communicated to

- Idiosyncrasies

- What else?

52 Nonstop Networking Tips (Practice over Time)

1. Give yourself permission to network. Maintaining a positive attitude is the first step to networking success.

2. Make a list of "opening lines" to use when meeting someone new. Use open-ended questions to create dialogue.

3. Develop a 20-second introduction about yourself. Practice it until it becomes spontaneous and natural. Create several for different audiences.

4. Do your research before attending an event or meeting. Learn the basics about the organization and the people likely to be there.

5. Have a list of "get to know you" questions." These go deeper than opening line questions; they help you to get know the interests of the person you just met.

6. Keep a journal of "small talk" topics, such as current events, industry topics, books, movies, community topics, and the like.

7. Set a goal for every event or meeting you attend. A good goal is to meet two new people; make a connection; and send a follow-up note, call, or email.

8. Smile when meeting people, entering a room, or talking on the phone. A smile is the first step in building rapport. Smile for 10 seconds when you enter a room. (Research says that this makes you more approachable.)

9. Look the other person in the eye. It shows that you are focused on the conversation and interested in what the other person is saying. The eyes are the windows of the soul.

10. Listen with care. Be aware of what the other person is saying instead of thinking about what you will say next. *Listen* has the word *silent* in it—silence your mind to focus and listen.

11. Learn to remember names. This skill will set you apart. Listen carefully when the name is said, repeat it in the conversation, and create a mind picture that will help you associate the person with the name.

12. Give compliments. Make a goal to look for positive attributes and give five compliments a day. Make sure they are sincere.

13. Make a list of the key people in your industry or profession that you would like to meet. Determine what organizations, places, and people you know that might help you connect.

14. Reconnect with four people a week. Call a client, prospect, colleague, and friend you haven't spoken with for several months.

15. Join a networking group and attend the meetings. Practice techniques such as your 20-second introduction, and keep expanding your circle.

16. Research and join industry and professional groups. Go to two meetings, meet two people, and set up two follow-up meetings before you make your decision to join. (2-2-2 Theory)

17. Join service groups such as your chamber of commerce, local Rotary chapter, or fund-raising organizations. Follow your interests in this matter. Join for the sake of giving, not getting.

18. Follow your interests. Remember, you need like-minded people in your network.

19. Volunteer, write an article, or join a committee in your organization. Becoming known helps you meet people and develop relationships faster and more profitably than just attending meetings. Be involved.

20. Send three handwritten notes a day. Send these to people in your network to say thank you or congratulations, send an article of interest, extend an invitation, or just keep in touch. Use found time during the day, and make these short and simple. Carry note cards and Forever stamps with you.

21. Write an article or newsletter to send to your contacts. This promotes your business and also helps you keep in touch with your contacts and stay on their radar.

22. Send gifts. Remember those who help you, or remember a special occasion for those in your network. Develop a list of reliable vendors of unique gift items for these occasions. Think of the person, and send a gift that you picked especially for him or her.

23. Use premiums that remind people of you and your business. Look for something that will be appreciated and that will keep your name in front of others.

24. Follow up within 24 hours of a meeting to say, "Nice to meet you" and "Thanks for your time and consideration," and to set another meeting.

25. Call within two weeks of suggesting another meeting. "Let's do lunch" is not an effective networking technique. Make it happen and set the date.

26. Send materials or information promised—on time or sooner than promised.

27. Thank your contact for a referral and let him or her know what happened. Keep your contacts in the loop.

28. Become a resource for others. Give generously of your time and expertise.

29. Look for unique and creative ways to have face time. Be creative and think outside the box.

30. Remember birthdays and special occasions, and send a card.

31. Review your list of contacts on a regular basis, and make sure it is revised and updated.

32. Develop a system to keep in touch with everyone in your network on a regular basis. As your list grows, divide it into categories and have a contact plan.

33. Maintain the system. It should work for you; you should not have to work for your system.

34. Collect information about each contact besides the basic information. This includes interests, family, awards and promotions, special dates, how you met, and other pertinent facts.

35. Determine the contact's preferred method of communication: phone, email, text, social media, in person. Note this on the person's database record.

36. Make and keep notes about each meeting with each contact. Refer to these when following up or before the next connection with him or her.

37. Have a system for keeping track of your contacts.

38. Enter information about a new contact within 24 hours of your meeting.

39. Answer all communications within 24 hours, even when you are on the road.

40. When you're out of the office, let people know with a message on your phone and an automatic email message.

41. Every day, send an email to someone in your database whom you have not been in touch with recently.

42. Once a week, go through your contact list and connect with three people to say hello.

43. Once a month, have lunch with a friend, colleague, or client.

44. At a company function, set a goal to sit next to someone new and get to know him or her. Also plan a method to follow up with them.

45. When making a phone call feels uncomfortable, use a script and practice until it becomes natural.

46. Begin with a compliment. This is a wonderful way to start a conversation when you might not know what to say to break the ice. Be sincere.

47. When a conversation gets off the topic you want to talk about, use a "bridge," such as "That reminds me of..." to get back on track.

48. Attend meetings with a purpose. Have a specific goal in mind when attending an industry event or other traditional networking meeting. It could be to meet the speaker or reconnect with a new client or prospect.

49. Set a time limit. When spending an entire meeting with an unknown group seems daunting, give yourself permission to leave after a specific time—at least one hour.

50. Send articles and interesting research electronically to keep in touch.

51. Give yourself a reward for your continual networking practice, whether for attending an event or reconnecting with someone from your past.

52. Network on the Internet with professional search engines.

ABC's of Life Networking

A Take **action**, monitor your **attitude**, be an **ambassador** of the firm, create **advocacy**

B **Belong** to groups (industry, professional, special interest, client focused)

C Call your **clients** and **contacts—connect**

D **Deliver** what you say immediately and consistently

E **Empathy**, **execute**, **evolution**, **eyes**, and **ears** (opened), **Engage** in the process

F **Friendly** approach, **find** opportunities to be in touch

G **Goals, give, grow**

H **Humor** and **help**—they go hand in hand

I **Initiate** and show **interest**

J **Join** and be involved

K **Keep** in touch with your contacts' preferred method of communication

L   **Listen** and **learn**

M   **Motivate** yourself to keep the process going, think like a **marketer**

N   **Nurture** your relationships

O   Be **open**, ask **open-ended** questions, take the **opportunity** to learn from all

P   **Process, plan, practice**

Q   Set your **quota**—**quality** versus **quantity**

R   **Research**, be a **resource, refer** others

S   **Strategy, system, success**

T   **Trust** takes **time**

U   **Understand** first, everyone is **unique**

V   **Versatility** counts

W   **Write** to stay in touch

X   **XO**—really like the people in your continual networks

Y   Focus on the other **you**—what are your contacts' interests?

Z   **Zero** in on all opportunities and possibilities with new and nurtured connections

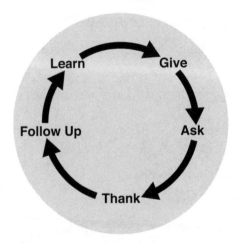

Figure A3-1 The Golden Circle of Strategic Networking

Index

thank you chains, 206, 244

thinkers versus feelers, 131

thinking of you notes, 220

third eye, 98

toolkits, 87

    intangible, 58-59

    tangible, 59-60

traits of common personality types, 129

travel tips, 151

trust, 145, 169

    building, 207-209

U

Unique Promise of Value, 143-144

uniqueness, communicating, 68

universal networks, 32-33

V

visual, communication styles, 126

visual stories, remembering names, 100

voicemails, etiquette, 165

volunteering, 46-47

W

Walmart, 252

Walton, Sam, 252

web, writing for, 184-185

WII-FM (What's in It for Me), 154

wish you were here notes, 220

women versus men

    bonding, 130-131

    communication, 132-133

    thinkers versus feelers, 131

worst things people do while networking, 154-155

writing

    articles, 47-48

    introverts, 176

    for publications and the web, introverts, 184-185

writing utensils, 60

Y-Z

You (focusing on), 103